25 NP

Business Management in Twenty-Second Century

Author – Dr. C Vasanta Madhavi

Disclaimer: The publisher or author or printers claim no responsibility for any mistakes that may have crept in inadvertently.

Thanks to…

All business professionals who keep sharing their views and opinions with me at all junctures

All my faculty members and teachers to make me think rationally and logically

All my family members & friends for providing review feedback and smidgens of doubts to doubt on myself

My mother for supporting me, my brother for trusting me and my father for criticizing me

Hope you enjoy it as well…

Appetizer

The book gives a sneak peek into the changing business conditions and strategies to tackle them. Each condition brings with itself a new challenge. Each new challenge seeks a new strategy. The solutions are no more within the opportunities but outside the opportunities. The opportunities arise out of earlier solutions and the new solutions give rise to another set of problems and challenges. Conditions are no more just dynamic but unpredictable and hi-tech. Business can be conducted online, offline, virtual, in-store, part-time, full-time, customer-centric, seller-centric, employee-centric, channel-centric, client-centric, innovation-centric, technology-centric, product-centric, service-centric, location-based, revenue-oriented, growth-oriented, market-oriented or sales-oriented. Business margins are not based on products or volumes but more on customization and technological usability. Profits are directly related to product usability. Costs and revenues have to be optimum. Traditional business secrets are carried forward to modern business conditions but with a capability to dynamically translate them into newer strategies with completely unknown measures. Measures themselves become means to achieving success in growth and sustenance of business.

Contents

Chapter 1

Changing Market Dynamics

Business is no more defined by brands or names of companies. The needs of buyers have to be directly matched with the offering of sellers. It is a bi-directional flow between customers and sellers. Sellers gather products after different market researches, technological adaptations, and promotional strategies. Buyer had a set of distinct needs that need to be fitted against a single product rather than multiple. Markets react to innovation and buyer demand to bring out the optimum product at any given point in time. There are several unknown students, scholars, engineers, scientists, mathematicians, doctors, technicians, skilled professionals and regulators to understand user, innovate technology, manufacture product, compare with existing competitors, test usability, devise marketability and distribution, prevent exploitation or misuse.

Markets don't settle but continue to evolve by time and resources. Markets interact with one another based on location, sector, dependencies, demand, supply, factors, etc. Geographies encourage market-interaction out of variances in interest rates, currency fluctuations, cross-border or regional opportunities, pricing, primary-secondary stock trading, debt-equity bends, economic differences, and technological advancements. Sectorial interaction between markets happens due to allied, related, unrelated, interrelated, genesis of industries. This interaction will become more unpredictable in future. So far, accessories or supplies of products and expertise for services have been coming out of different sectors to satisfy the current needs of sector. Later, combinations of inter-usability will arise from vastly unrelated sectors to make use of reengineering, processing, innovating and evolving newer products unknown hitherto. Solar energy is gaining importance in all industries and not just household use like power as earlier. It is being put to more use in industry applications, school operations, field activities, etc. Such activities will become more of unrelated ones like technological adaptation itself. Tomorrow the cell chargers may be based on solar energy completely; battery cells may save solar energy to operate in power-crisis. They will be even more new uses like solar energy for vehicles, transportation or resource engineering of water, wind and trees. Markets across the globe interact because of meeting excess demand or supply requirements. The factors influencing or driving markets are interest rates, currencies, mergers, inter-continental trading and governmental activity. These are inherently different because of apparent difference in literacy levels, life-standards, personality-traits, evolution patterns within these nations. They are overcome with suitable policies encouraging cross-border trade, cultural product adaptations, technology gap-complexity, training facilities, global business. Interaction is facilitated by local-regional-global law, social and cultural adaptations, with the help of strategies and tactics to solve global challenges and differences acclimatizing businesses to meet needs of users from different locations from products at different locations. The supply-chain network of global business would have buyers in different locations using products and services based in different locations with the help of adaptation facilitated by technology. The global cloud servers give access to local geeks to adapt the technologies to their needs. Experts overseeing such transitions would be based out of diverse locations without necessarily being local or glocal always. Distribution of products is thus not an issue because the availability itself would be spot-based. The global unifying platform is the technology or the basic technology because technology itself is different in use and capability for different geographies. There will be local adaptation of products, culture-based usability of services, but global factorization and fraternization. The defining features would be globally same. The manufacturing processes would be uniform across the boundaries. Payment and settlement will be a mix of local and glocal mechanisms. Currency options will be more availed based on buyer status, credit card access, product laundering. Product laundering means that the person in one country may choose to buy from another though the adaptation may not be completely suitable. A buyer likes a product from one country for one or two of the five features. She buys it online and chooses to pay in currency of yet a different country for making arbitrage currency gains. This is more possible because all the channel partners of a product will be based in all parts of the world. Hence the transaction itself will be multi-channel network of complex sub-activities across the globe giving the maximum benefit to buyer and seller. Seller will then be able to sell more because the buyer decides purchase based on multiple factors. Each feature itself is a conglomerate of different cultural adaptations thus making the product truly global. The world of business becomes global day-by-day, yet there are several restrictions and preconditions to it. Markets are facilitated and hampered by the same participants. Markets don't care about user emotions. Market sentiments are blind in many ways. Firstly, all activities are linked or interdependent due to which market uncertainty is unavoidable if one link behaves different from others. Secondly, markets are neutral. Economies don't know each other. Markets are logical. Markets understand only numbers and not the languages. Markets are not commanded over but markets are controllers of business. Businesses are all puppets in the hands of markets. Markets can sweep or raise economies because they are the lynch-pins between firms and economies. Winners learn from losers to help them with a third-party solution. The losers can be identified from the middle rather than waiting for the vertical chance. The pack of losers can be moved ahead so that the balance is not disturbed by being excess on sides and low on middle tranche. Markets cannot be forgotten for reasons of failure or slowdown because all markets are equal in the eyes of economic success. To get global economic success, all markets have to be strong. The strongest ones in the tail can push weak ones ahead so that the resource utility is max and any depletion or lack is immediately highlighted to the leader. Weak markets will be visible to strong markets in this way and also will look forward to success. Weak markets will learn to wait for other weaker markets to march ahead of them and let them fill in the dearth of resources or capabilities in weak markets. The leadership of strong markets is in their ability to continue with the innovation by being in the last. Being in the last won't stop them from foreseeing market progress. A possible revolution in the future will let strong markets change their guidance for weak markets. The guiding tactics for weak and strong markets will be consistent and not drastically different to keep them on the same line.

There are markets to facilitate range of trade and business among and within regions. The dynamics of business between markets are different and changing. Competitive laws are different among markets. Currencies operating within markets are different. Markets talk to each other solely on financial terms purely translating into numbers. Money is counted and not measured. Markets run on monetary terms and hence market success is also counted but not measured. On a firm level, money can be counted as less, more, positive or negative flow. Market success is binary and counted as 0 or 1. Economy can boom or go bust if market success is not 1 continuously or ever. Market that counts success continuously is emulated after. Market that counts failure continuously is treated as lagging behind. Markets don't interact with lagging ones. Markets shout success stories backed by numbers. Weak markets are exploited by strong markets or are left behind. Exploitation happens on labor, resources, technology, pricing, competitive cartels, monopolies, growth and expansion. Raw material and other capabilities are dragged out of weak markets by strong ones. Expansion happens if there is profit potential and not to explore opportunities. Governments intervene by offering incentives or discounts or exemptions to encourage weak markets towards strength. Arbitrage opportunities are exploited to suck weak markets out of strength. Cartels and monopolies develop into unhealthy competition nexus between strong and weak markets. Weak markets are prone in the future also but the market will be more adaptive to global changes. Strong markets are becoming more like big brothers holding the weak markets to guide them out of crisis. Thus the gap between poor and strong markets is bridged by cooperation rather than ousting. Market adjustments are fast in the modern world to accommodate other market's weakness or lessons or best practices. Markets respond to bail or learn from others. Keeping the markets constant or dormant is in a way not possible. Markets cannot be stable because technology is varying in them. Advanced technologies won't let weak markets get stable. Strong markets are constantly making adjustments for letting others with low technology participate in global war of business. Strong markets are also trying to be on the uptick in the market evolution. The war is between winners and losers and future is working on making losers as winners rather than eliminating them. The gain is in terms of returns from the investment already made as effort, time, resources, money or capabilities that get recovered after becoming winners. Winners are not made instantly but out of repeated learning from strong markets. In the case, winning markets don't race ahead in the race but stay in the last! Stay in the last and make sure that the markets in front of them are all running and strong. The weak links move ahead as and when strong leaders emerge in the front or weak markets emerge in between. Imagine a world where markets are all successful and strong. Innovation levels will be at the peak and such a world would never see depression or failure. Markets are dynamiting the barriers of unfruitful ventures and converting all into success with the help of global cooperation. The task is facilitated with the help of technology. Thus tomorrow's market success is in staying last in the queue to make the entire line strong. Strong Markets will stand in the end to monitor the rest. Weakest market will be in the front and lead the rest thus optimizing the speed of world economic progress without letting the strongest to vanish in the front without any clues for future. The model optimizes the use of resources too. Strong markets will progress only as much as that can enable weak ones to progress but not waste resources endlessly in uni-directional growth. Thus the progress will flow from back to front rather than top to bottom or front to end. Parallel progress is more widespread than vertical sequential progress. World is a globe and markets are all running behind one another so any sequence is not disturbing the circular world of money business. Strong markets are not running but pushing others ahead of them to make the business world a winner for the global economy. Markets never ignore technology and utilize technology to the benefit of bringing weak markets into growth. Wisdom is not in pulling the weak but pushing them forth. Business wisdom shows that the strong players have always overcome the weak in cases of industry evolution. However, the current pace of fastest growth does not allow for investments to be ignores. In that case all markets have to be winners. It's not to say that markets will accept a losing firm's products. But markets will help by innovating products to release a uniform pool of products at a given point in time to make the weak players strong. Strong players will show the way of success to the weak ones to overcome their weaknesses either by investing in Mergers & Acquisitions or short-term ventures. No company is without any asset. Every asset is equally valuable. All assets can be utilized to make the market a winner. The winning story is in taking the lessons from strong market and applies it to the weak markets to test their universality. If a best-practice is not versatile enough to mend a weak company, then it is not so. The weak companies need to become strong to make the market strong. The markets become strong to make the economy strong. Conversion of elimination into inclusion is not an easy task but time indicates so. It is a Herculean task to convert non-performers into performers. Non-performing economies can be lagging behind due to unfavourable market conditions like interest rates, volatilities, weak markets, and weak markets can be so due to cultural factors, resource limitations, failing firms, and weak firms can be so due to incompetent leadership, low-grade technology, and all of which are not unassailable. Technology and competent staff can convert weak into strong firms. Adaptive and agile culture in successful firms can convert weak into strong markets. Strong markets can convert weak into strong economies. Agile markets don't always change but enable change to come at right times and prevent change in wrong times. Agility is in responding to others and enabling them to change. Non-agility can be overcome with the help of agility and agility alone and thus agility can come with the help of responding to change and adapting to change. Ignoring change in wrong times and not responding to wrong signals is also agility. Agility lies in continuous momentum. Momentum is both moment and stability. Stability in the right time and motion in the inert times make markets agile along with the firms. Markets won't succumb to weak times if firms are agile. Some firms should respond and others shouldn't. Weak firms should respond to their weaknesses. Strong firms should respond to market weaknesses. The balance occurring due to agility will create an agile environment for the economy. Markets monitor the movements of firms and don't accept haphazard ones. Just responding for the sake of it is not agile. Agile markets display right movements from strong companies and momentum from weak ones. Markets are not averse to non-response provided it comes at the right time. Unaware companies and markets that do not understand the market dynamics hit the success only by chance. Success needs planning and business success is dependent solely on strategic planning. Market watches the players on how they time their entry, introductions, expansions, growth and other strategies. Market rewards the right players with success and the wrong ones a chance to change. Therefore we see firms closely watching others. Rivalry is not just taking over others but understanding the moves of other players and preparing counter-strategies. Markets are not bothered about who forms and executes strategies for companies. Today, markets are not giving importance to when and where but the results. Thus the responsibility of companies and businesses is to foresee the next steps for action in a successful business tomorrow and make it a success today. The changes in markets are multi-directional from firms and economies. A market upraises and leads to changes in interest rates. An interest change leads to immediate market and firm reaction. Market reactions enforce change in firms' response and strategies. Sectorial performances lead to changes in economic policies. Industry uprising is directly related to market upheaval. Dynamic markets predict economic changes and warn industry of the forthcoming challenges. Macro changes can bring in important challenges for the firms. Micro economic reactions are consequences and causes of industry strategies. Dynamic markets act and react oblivious of the other economic and industry changes. They are both proactive and reactive in times of need. A reactive strategy prevents firms from making slowdown. A proactive strategy is aimed at achieving growth. Markets produce and affect economic and firm level strategies. Markets do not make strategies but interact with economy and firm level strategies. Firms can make strategies at market level. Economies can make strategies at market level. But markets never make strategies for firms or for economies. Markets are day watchers. Economies and firms are night dogs. Markets do not function during nights literally. But the impact is seen overnight when market changes favourably or unfavourably under given circumstances for or against a sector or economy. Economies can topple markets and markets can topple firms. Markets are inter-linkages for companies and economies.

Markets encourage companies to work with the economic parameters as changes occur. Markets encourage economies to experiment with sectorial policy changes. Today's markets balance dynamics in such a way that economy and firms can interact on real-time basis without loss of delay in communication. Earlier the ripple effect or chain effect used to take decades for markets to penetrate into firms or to economies. The entire evolution of firms and industry is now taking only few years. In five to ten years, companies either shut down or merge with others if performance is not winning. That too, in a rapidly changing world economy, firm or market interacts with others on a daily basis. Future will see this interaction getting more streamlined and proactive rather than cause-and-effect flow. Markets change according to firms' performance and economic leaders' decisions. Successful economies are those that create healthy markets by growing firms.

Chapter 2

Types of Business Scenarios

Business scenarios are based on the goal, resources, achievement, investment and returns. These are totally intrinsic to a company. But they are the major drivers of changing business scenarios. External drivers are competition, innovation, markets, govt. Business scenarios differ on the basis of how much target is achieved, by what means and at what cost in comparison to competitors. The combinations of all these parameters give scenarios for forecasting, deriving best practices, success factors, failing lessons, etc. Growth, saturation, expansion, decline, leadership, bankruptcy are all different scenarios in business. Changes sometimes occur so rapidly that these scenarios can't be predicted. Technological changes can be at nano-fraction in tomorrow's business and business scenarios have to be managed multiple at a time. Business conditions are anyway volatile and uncertain; combine the technological uncertainty and industrial volatility to get the most liquid business conditions. Governments form policies once in a year or multiple times in a term. Industries can form strategies every quarter or month depending on players' dynamism. Players can decide to spurn products depending on their R&D or management capabilities. Most of the moves of the players are responses of others'. Response is not known as the move is not unknown until the firm announces or does it. 50% of the strategies of firms can hence be taken as ad hoc. The other 50% are related to the internal goals and mission-vision and hence can be taken as 'defined'. Defined strategies like those related to employees, corporate goals, markets, core business are all common to any player in the industry. Market is 100% volatile and movements are unpredictable because of dependency on micro, macro, industry level movements. Market movements are multi-directional protected by economy and challenged by industry.

Industry obeys market signals but firms are at their free will to implement strategies. Strategies are aligned more towards individual firm's growth rather than industry or market. Economy takes market signals as motives for protecting industry or economy and warning for aligning policies.

Some of the business scenarios are –

- Industry stage – firms may be at different levels of growth, maturity, saturation. Decline is not important since firms are not in existence then. The stage refers to technology or firm's leadership and both of which keep changing. In future, business scenarios will shift rapidly among themselves. Conglomerate firms would be bound to display activity like takeovers, or joint ventures.
- Technology orientation – can create a business scenario in itself. Technology is not as easily adopted in its best version as it sounds. Companies adopt technology in nascent, advanced or even out-dated stage. Future will see more technology facets to combine firms with different

technological capabilities to bring out the best in and out of the industry. Outsourcing will convert into collaboration.

- Innovation – can create intrinsic and extrinsic scenario for industries, firms and markets. Sectors can be in one scenario, firms can fall under a different state of innovation, or markets can work on different trends of innovation.
- Competition – scenarios are in market leadership, growth and advancement. Some players may be in the competitive state of being leaders, other may be in the last rung, another may be in the process of climbing up the leadership rung, and even others may be in the exit mode.

Whatever be the combination of state in the above scenarios, firms can form independent strategies, irrespective of industry progress or market signals. The first two are intrinsic and last two are extrinsic. However, depending on the strategic impact and responses of market, the intrinsic can become extrinsic business scenario and vice versa.

Goals, strategies, measures, can change with or without any major market intervention within firms. Business conditions change without much uncertainty but as step-by-step process. Market reactions are uncertain. Firm operations are certain. Combining the uncertain and certain conditions gives rise to more business scenarios. Combination of volatility and non-volatility business scenarios can create further scenarios that are mostly volatile. Business scenarios that are weak in technology cannot excel whatever strategies are used for the growth. Business scenarios that are demanding in resources, technologies, strategies, opportunities, can create challenges for companies to propel them into growth. Business scenarios can reflect individual firm's or market's state. One business scenario can be common for multiple firms or it can be unique to each firm. Business scenarios can apply to many firms or markets. New business conditions can give rise to new scenarios. Each scenario would have different parameters like interest rate, key drivers, competition, technology to define the inputs and outputs. Inputs form a scenario for the firms and markets to react with their outputs. Every firm sustains under a business scenario or a set. A new firm operates under the business scenarios of forming its entity for playing with competition and satisfying customers. Another firm runs under circumstances of rigorous compliance and price-breaking monopoly. Some other firms follow cartelized markets and free competition.

Steps are taken by firms to understand, beat, forecast, scenarios. Participants are firms, markets, governments and to go a step further, employees, customers, shareholders, investors, suppliers, marketers, distributors and agencies are all participants in defining the business scenarios. External components and internal drivers equally contribute to the ways of operating business under different scenarios. Multiple scenarios can combine into a single one if the triggers are common over time. Single scenario can split into multiple if the factors are diverse and multi-dimensional. Companies gain versatility in the way they deal with their business scenarios. Market concurs or differs from companies' approach towards the business scenario. Gaining an edge over others is possible by competing over a business scenario rather than a strategic move. Business moves can create very specific and situational strategies but business scenarios can create imitable and best practice strategies. Markets run with business and economy in parallel. Markets take cues from economy and vice versa. Markets give signals to businesses and dictate terms but firms cannot dictate terms to markets. Companies can take signals from markets and industries can send collective signals to markets. It is more or less a one-way interaction between markets and firms. It is bi-directional communication between markets and economy. Several business scenarios arise and can be created out of market signals. Each signal can be perceived to be representative of more than one scenario depending on which way firms move. Response to signals can be bi-dimensional from firms. The response in turn generates new scenarios and more responses from competitors. Markets create reaction for the firms through tickers or another trigger for change. Change is continuous. Companies should not play around with market rules because business scenarios cannot function if any of the rules of the game is violated. Dumb firms that do not respond to changing business scenarios stay stuck within a given static business scenario without making much improvement in the industry. Companies that add value to industry beyond their own stay in a progressive business scenario because they can gauge and forecast future scenario fast. Industries contribute in the creation of business scenario and each firm gets as it deserves. A tough firm does not land an easy business scenario. A start-up does not land in a tough business scenario. As firms grow, they can choose to handle a tougher business scenario than earlier. Such proactive firms are agile and move fast in the market making progress in each scenario. Big firms should not try to exploit small firms in scenarios of adversity or progress. Some firms grow fast and become big to avoid exploitation. Big firms face pressure of size vs. performance. Happy firms are those with agile ways of shifting from one scenario to another. Companies can take help of other companies and market resources in facing a business situation. Business situations can land firms in crisis or prosperity depending on the time lag in appropriately responding to competitors and customers. Competitors create business scenarios for other players for short-term. Customers create business scenarios for long-term. Right products under given business scenarios can give companies an edge over others. Business scenarios can churn out innovation and new customer segments depending on the amount of business intensity shown in handling a given condition using the latest technology.

Business conditions emerge according to technological innovations and regulatory changes. Firms face challenging situations according to their capabilities. Business environment rewards those firms with excelling beyond their capabilities and market expectations. Other firms lag behind if they underutilize the skills of company stakeholders. Employees bring in specialized skill, customers bring in third-party advisory skill, suppliers bring in best-practices skill, likewise all participants in any value-chain bring in some or the other set of skills. Dynamic skills can be developed if companies function with agility. Agility in accepting as-is, predicting to-be, optimizing skills, and getting results out of dynamic skills create business dynamism for companies to flourish. Future is going to see availability of all skills like a pool, from which agile companies would develop capabilities to address precise needs of market. New business scenarios can be forfeited by winning in the existing ones to make the most in the market. Growth and leadership come from being correctly-timed to precisely - strategized to accurately-measured to galvanizing-position in the market. Correct timing of products and launches is important for reigning over competition. Precise strategies are important for winning over customers as well as meeting governmental agency deadlines. Employee precision and stakeholder satisfaction are important for achieving market results. Numbers and facts are important for establishing leadership in the market. In times of excellence and bankruptcy, companies look ahead for the help of government agencies or collaborators. Business scenarios are passing clouds leaving value-chain-participant and stakeholder relationships to aid the companies in adverse times or progressive. The takeaway from each business scenario should be aimed at sustaining and improving the business growth statistics by extracting new skills, technologies, capabilities, relationships, connections, references, networks, channels, customers, values, goals, investments, ventures, competitors and markets. New skills promote employees in the market and their credibility adds to the company performance. New technologies are always capable of giving innovative capabilities to the firms. Technologies bring in more attention of market and competitors thus adding to the reputation. Technologies can be upgraded and are never a waste of investment as they bring in results in a short-term. New capabilities like offerings, services, products, geographies, customers, methodologies, etc. can be acquired by new interactions between channel partners while handling a business scenario. New relationships can be formed with various stakeholders, investors, customers, value-chain participants, government bodies, competitors, collaborators, sponsors, employees and almost everyone involved in business in terms of redefined expectation, new targets or new policies.

Chapter 3

Sales in Tomorrow's Markets

Future is going to see extremely and radically different sales. Online sales are going to get popular and basic. More sales would occur through vending machines and bill boards on roadsides. Vending machines would handle or dispose of serious stuff like pizzas, furniture, clothing, shoes, cakes etc. Bill boards would take in credit-card payment to sell out instantly small items or through home-delivery or store-pick-up of big items. Clothing, accessories and shoes would be more dispensable through virtual stores where tailor made items can be sent after virtual try-ons. Displays and showrooms would be replaced with virtual kiosks. Screens would be more of air panels and electric eye glass controls. Interactive open air showrooms with personalised online websites or group-site…

Each world citizen would own a group-site. A group-site is a personalized collection of all relevant websites only to a person who own that website. In simple terms, each one of us would log into our own website – a single one instead of multiple ones as we do now. A single website that would collate all our websites and give us a single access-check for security is group-site. In the next century, geeks won't have time to open 10 windows on a tablet for mails, travel, entertainment, banking, payment of bills, gadget recharge, doctor appointment booking, food orders, shoes, and forget college fee site or let the device crash. A group-site www.adam.com say opens a single window entry using biometrics or eye-retina match for all sites relevant to Adam – different tabs showing cars (to check insurance), houses (to pay rent), personal care (clothes, bags, gels), office (work emails), extra paraphernalia tabs like family (kids' fee, etc.), adventure (booking trips), contests (to participate in sports, competitions globally), news events (for all preferred alerts). The list can go on according to the personal preferences. The advantage is that of privacy and security along with precision and accuracy. A person would not miss anything. Nor would she waste time on browsing and searching among unnecessary sites. Restrictions can be easy for parents to regulate movies or other content. The groupie is like a home within home for every citizen in the world. The entire identity and rights or responsibilities can be linked too. Voting can be conducted. Every person uses the same home computer. There is no risk of rigging or forcible voting. Hacking systems can be evaded with the highest levels of security which would be prevalent in the next century for sure. A lot more stuff can be done on fun and serious sides. The person's location, tracking, contact details would be made available through the group-site id and distributed to all family-friends via jet apps. Jet apps are the assumed names of apps following online and mobile apps, after this century. Jet apps need air screens to operate and not any device like a mobile or laptop. Most of the gadgets would take the form of air screens in the next century. They would eliminate the need for carrying additional devices. A handy blue-ray or advanced Nano-wave headset or rather a simple earplug can carry the chip holding the entire life of a person. Transactions of purchase, sale, bookings, emails, etc. all can be done on a thin airspace using the personal banking or virtual card details. The whole process of sale would take the shape of click-n-get. A single click would complete the payment and shipping. The buyer would simply get it delivered to home or pick it from the nearest warehouse. Goods would not be sold through showrooms as much as through air-warehouse. The booking would be on air, the dispatch would be on warehouse. Or even the warehouse points can be replaced with the vendor location. Anybody can sell anything. I have an extra pen, so I sell it on air. A store sells best pens. I choose my next pen from there on air. The sale is the final point and hence is being stressed in the book. However the entire panorama of offerings of products, services and supply-chain is going to go through a macro-evolution making it a micro-event boiling down to just the evident sale. Services would move at a breath-taking pace. Hence the only criterion of success is the buyer-will. If the buyers buy a product, then the company is a success otherwise not.

Chapter 4

Trade of Opportunities-Solutions

Each problem in the next century would become an opportunity for business and buyers. The essence is that the literacy and technology levels would be at pinnacle and as such there would be no failing ideas because every idea would be worked till success. The business world would become a pool of opportunities and solutions. Not every industry would be able to sustain the speed and pace of the next century. But most of them would converge or merge to form allied sectors rather than totally getting wiped away. If next century sees no need of a laptop, the industry would be that of refurbished components that after R&D can be used in Nano-devices or Nano-chips aiding the Nano-industries like finger-top or dwarf-cars. Finger-tops are sleek versions of palm-tops, and can be held over like a keychain. Dwarf cars are Nano-auto-vehicles that are compact and can run for duo thus saving all space and pollution on roads. Corporate houses would not be based on large spaces; rather the space would be leased to employees for housing of the exploding population on a non-exploding planet (or may be some of us would move to MARS). All business houses would be virtual offices with operations fully on-air. Online would be converted into on-air (onair) group-sites where only stations would be those of manufacturing and storage. Thus profits would largely accrue from the cut-down cost of office per se. The virtual networks would be replaced with onair groups for business, social media, sports, etc. These are different levels of communication, horizontal, vertical and diagonal. A horizontal group would be like that of quality, insurance or social media. A vertical onair group would be that of banks, auto, toys or coffee. Diagonal group would be that of food, confectionery, or business that is common for handling quality as well as product versions. Businesses would roll on opportunities and solutions like two sides of a coin plus on the edge of technological excellence. The world would be truly 3-dimensional because of the fast transition through business excellence, opportunity assessment and solution adoption. A business would be more like a family than a commercial enterprise. The opportunities would be generated by market and customers; and the solutions would be spurned by user community and geeks. The technology itself would be redefined by the robotics based on the concurrent usage and preference feedback. Statistics of market-user-technology trio would create a win-win situation for companies, customers and geeks. Geeks would emerge as a separate community because technology would govern the world (business also), and they would be from companies, customers and non-customers.

The opportunity-solution-technology trio would be creating a multi-dimensional world for ages to come. The single dimension that has survived so far is the solution or the products or items right from barter age till now. The current involvement of customers in business groundswell has created a 2-D world with lot of opportunities from non-customers also. The advent of technology as harbinger of business is soon set to give rise to another world with 3-D business. The initiation has happened in the form of virtual stores but is still to go a long way with Nano technologies in enabling the world business tango on the technology. The next dimension that would be added seems to be time. Technology would create tranches of time for each citizen. Business would be governed by time zenith via technological brilliance. Time governance would be nothing but aligning the life of every global citizen to her time-preference. Products and services would run according to her preference whether behind or ahead of times. Feedback would eliminate or enhance recurrences or re-preferences by others.

Technologies would be auto-reinvented by advanced schematic or neural robotics to be always on the next century. The pace of lifestyle and business would rather be left to the time to throw the imagination. Buyers and sellers won't be existent any more. The world would resemble the earliest Ice-age in terms of business in that every business channel would be non-formalized. Technology would transition leadership into time. One would get what one wants instantly. Rather the business would be hundred years ahead of the globe. The citizens would simply choose from the options and enable further evolution merely by being the part of the crowd. No deliberate attempt would be needed for evolution or feedback. It would the age of super-jet-speed on land!

Chapter 5

Rainbow - Customers, Employees, Suppliers, Processors, Traders, Government, Associations/ Agencies

Business in the coming decades is only going to be more and more exciting than yesterday. It is nothing short of movies like Terminator, Matrix series. Everything would be streamlined. The employees, bots, machines and tools would all be humanised or 'deviced'. Humans would take more help from robots as employees. Robots would take more help from human emotions as mechanised forerunners. The world of business is divulging all its secrets to customers to convert itself from being a grey or black-and-white world to rainbow of stakeholders. If butterflies in one country can bring in rain in another then the rain is going to bring a rainbow of colours for the stock-world to respond in a much more enigmatic way than ever. A market reaction in a remote location is going to bring in tremendous change world over. Customers in different locations would give different responses – positive and negative for the same reaction. Employees would be responsible for multiple companies. The skills would be divided over companies rather than wasting over a single skill on a firm. An employee can work 25% of his time with a skill in demand from Confectionery Company. She can contribute to nano-chips and semi-conductors firm 50% of her time and to automobiles firm 25% of her time. Skills would be hired rather than employees thus making employment a less burdensome task. Suppliers would not compete against companies but for companies. Every supplier would be strong in a supply-chain area so that the strengths would be supplied by the respective supplier. This is true of not only supplier but also of all the value-chain partners. Processors or other participants would be integrated in such a manner that the companies won't be any more distinguished by activities but by customers. Each technology would be a skill owned by a company. The services and activities would be distributed among firms in such a way that every firm finds its utility in the market and is able to compete for leadership. It would be a business of equals but still unequal competing with one another. In a way, the corporate socialism, and communism, etc. would all be replaced by corporatism, neither commercial nor non-profitable but somewhere in the middle of the line as excellence being championed by corporate. Business world would have no time to waste over experimenting with failures and trials. It would be only innovation that would back the business in every corner of the world. Governments would act more as checks rather than facilitators. Everything would be facilitated by technology and associations would administer verification points to ensure the welfare of society and safeguarding of environment.

The inputs from all corners of the business would be aligned and put to best use in such a way that all feedback would be useful for business intelligence. Each level would add colour to the business thus making it an enviable age for corporates. All businesses would compete for generating the rainbow of value-chain components thus making optimizing a pre-requisite. Value-chain optimization would create the most optimum business scenario and rainbow would create the next level of delight for the business. Thus after delighting the customers, it is the business that gets delighted in such a way that it paves way for future customer delight. The various parameters like efficiency, effectiveness, performance, time-to-market, time-to-delivery, time-to-launch, profitability, return, inventory, stocking, turnovers, flows, manufacturing processes, bottlenecks and testing would all be optimized without scope for further improvements. This is where business would reach its zenith. Like all rainbows, the one here is also a result of the rain of inputs (positive, negative, future suggestions) that make business excellence a continuous process.

Chapter 6

Packaging technology into powerful gadgets – Independence Day

Technology is like free electricity that must be used in various forms to be of utility. We have the forms, matter and needs. Forms are different devices that are needed for the future. May be, a radio for communicating from Mars to Jupiter, or a blu-man to replace the DVD-man, or a gadget to watch videos from pen, or a remote control car to drive kids to school from being at home- all are future devices. We need human beings as operators of robotics and not for any intelligent applications. To eliminate human intervention to this large an extent, all technology needs to be converted into matter – computer codes, radio waves, infra-RFID-Nano components, etc. The needs are clear or would be popping up soon to drive the matter and forms, and vice versa. Customers expect as much as they can visualize or foresee or imagine. All future human efforts would be directed towards honing imagination skills. We are all geniuses in one way or the other but we need to imagine the intelligently. Einstein could have missed the train if his imagination were to be confined to home-work completion and topping the school. Edison would not have been remembered for his imaginative world of newspapers delivery or ways of making his mother's life easier. They all imagined for the future of the world and made it to there. Technology would take off the headache of automation and free human brains to imagine the future of mankind along with business. Powerful gadgets would define the future of future business. The steps taken by technology would have spiralling effect in rolling most of the new products for a great part of the future. Meanwhile, our imaginative geeks would bring in more ideas for enlivening the world of technology in coming centuries. Time would be such that those who imagine alone can excel. Businesses would do research, innovation and development as a process.

Employees or stakeholders or contributors with imagination can trigger new developments for technology. Self-driving technological advancements would be common but man can use imagination to be the master. Frankenstein cannot imagine beyond human capabilities as it is a product of human audacity. Thus human dominance can be sustained over technology with the help of imagination. One person in each company that can imagine the development of its technology, further evolution, forthcoming progress and new products can take business world to unknown heights. More imaginations and imaginative people can be technical assets on their own to win the business peaks. Products can be imaginative to the extent of self-evolution or logical improvements that can be auto-executed by products.

The journey started with the transfer of products and services across the borders by water, air or road.

Cross-border trader was simple. A product was ported elsewhere, with all else remaining same. Then the journey transitioned to trade between borders on a more specific basis of transferring people who made the products. Manufacturers now understood multiple regions and preferences to make better allied products to regions. But the limitation was that of the number of regions or states that the worker understood. Currency was different, pricing varied, functionality was totally different. A US car was not used on Indian roads nor was an Indian laptop charger used in UK. The products were branded as imported or export quality. Definite conditions were set for payment, availability and licensing. The advent of technology now makes it easier than earlier to make products made in one region, to be available at another region, to be sold in another, to be used in another, to be distributed in yet another region to be adapted elsewhere on different currencies at different times. The complexity is not as long-lived as apparent here. The time gap and currency gaps are no more visible. Transaction is seamless. Shipment is short. Feedback is instant. The very technological benefits create a challenging environment to necessitate radically innovative products to live that speed of product life cycle. As we understand global users are from different regions based in one or several places. The product is one that caters to different sets of users. The currencies are multiple that facilitate the transaction. The language is itself deciding for making the product usable whether in user-manuals or purchase-sale initiation through decision process. The packaging of technology into devices, articles, gadgets, items, things, is important because it is a combination of power-mechanism-feature into a tangible and usable object. The object is of a certain perception-expectation measure. The user should be excited and eager to use it as many times as possible and desired. Therefore it is no more a technology but a part of our life-system where the user interacts with the used and vice-versa. The used never interacts with the user so far. The razor does not interact with the shaver. The gentleman has to power it, charge it, and press it against the chin to use it. The razor is dormant until the user applies it. The trigger or button facilitates the use of razor in different parts of the country, but does not interact with the users. The next phase of journey is this very part of user-used interaction. The products will be built to meet global standards in as concise manner as possible if the product itself can adapt based on technology set within it. It is a combination of artificial intelligence, neural networks and robotics. Robotic science or robotic engineering deals with competing with humans *in terms of intelligence and logic. Rationale behind decisions runs by emotions and logic. Robotics is mastering the emotions part too. However logic itself is not complete, and will never be complete as long as new and innovative needs and products come up. Emotions will be defined but the combinations of emotion-logic will be infinite to be accommodated in robotics. Scientists are working on how to make a self-innovating robot that constantly redefines technology itself with no or less human intervention. Artificial intelligence is building up artificial neural combinations to emulate our brain in a robot. The chances are fair that they won't get headaches if random combinations run into effect. So medicines won't be needed for robots unless another twist develops to accommodate even the human diseases resulting out of emotions! That's again a different group of researchers breaking their heads upon.*

Research reports in everyday newspapers show as many contradictions as one can imagine. One report reveals chocolate's or cocoa's morale-boosting capacity. Another report talks about its thought-hampering process. Research of course should talk of both good and bad sides. What if a gadget talks to you, changes it and interacts with you? What if your pen asks you what to twirl or write on the paper before you use it? What if you can ask your pen on how to change a colour? What if you can share your feedback with the pen itself and it changes itself or repairs itself without you having to visit a store or paying extra for it? Artificial intelligence is not about automation but automation in the right time. A business cannot be brought into establishment and maturity through saturation in a day or two. It goes through the transition that takes millions of hours to form the business as a successful entity by incorporating goals and sentiments of multiple others. The stakeholders cannot ask for products to be converted into revenues in a month or two. It takes years and decades to gel with customers' needs. Therefore companies today are building automatic intelligence systems into their products whether a memory chip or a laptop. The devices can monitor themselves like terminator and repair or upgrade the versions. They can become non-operational or self-destroy after a given period of expiry or set of conditions. Siemens is working on a laboratory of machines to come up with robotic elements that can be fitted into various computers and medicinal equipment. These devices are ahead of RFID technologies and can recreate intelligent diagnosis, operations and maintenance process. They can regenerate source code and logic in machinery according to user needs and operator feedback overtime. The machines can also repair themselves *without much manual intervention. The branch of*

neural networks deals with intelligence and logic

which businesses prefer in their products. Products

and services are being used by buyers and their

feedback is instantly taken into account by the used

through the uses, types of uses, frequency of use and

features being often used. Neural networks create

combinations of activities and record the best one for

each user based on usage. How does the user hold

the cell phone whether with right or left hand? The

navigation is adjusted according to gestures and

movements of the user. Neural networks cannot

replace human logic but use human habits to frame

logic. This is not creating but recreating logic and

adapting the products to usage. Marketing is oriented

for usage and not user. Users may be different and

many but usage patterns are important for any object.

The patterns can be recorded against each user of a

product using biometrics or other identification security. Business organizations are now giving importance to user security along with safety. It is no more a majority for business but individual poll that matters for business success. Each and every customer is important. Technology innovators and R&D labs should understand this very well and undertake innovation that is user-centric rather than business-centric. Customer segments are no more going to be the determining factors of revenues but individual customers are going to gain increasing importance in the future. Business in 2100 won't say that customer segments are tapped to the extent of 80% or unexploited segments need to be covered. Companies in 2200 are not going to be dependent on categories of customers. All sectors will vie for every single customer. Nobody is going to be let as a non-customer. Every individual will gain the importance as a customer for every firm. The businesses are going to become more and more customer-centric rather than mission-centric. The participation of customers will be multi-faceted in every company's success. A customer is not going to be the direct buyer or user per se. Companies will spread the scope of their activities to all customers in order to attract their involvement and collaboration in business success. Markets won't be left alone to perform based on firms' operations. Customers will contribute equally to the performance of markets. They would get involved in all activities like mission-vision, operations, success planning, strategic orientation, marketing, sales, distribution, and even profit-sharing. The entry to exit journey will all be open for customers and therefore each customer will be key to the formation of success for a company in 2100's. The markets will vie for customer participation because customers will be *more informed than the companies. Employees would also become customers for companies because they would bring in more customers from outside. Groups of customers or segments can create their own entities to channelize products for use. A single customer can create her own pool of companies for meeting her individual and family needs. The virtual existence of companies can make it possible for us to own our suppliers and sellers. Customers can create their own supply chains and channels for customized offerings. The flexibility would be promoted by technologies rather than companies. Companies would be using or applying technologies by default rather than by choice. Firms of next century would be automated to a large extent. Monopolies would be run by customers. Cartels would be owned by customers. Competition would be driven from customers rather than other companies. Yesteryears' virtual reality of* customer kingship would be translated into reality in the next century corporate. As we see, we are progressing from a customer is a king – to customer is a partner – to customer is the God. Employees are indirect customers of companies. Without their buying the company, outside buyers won't become customers of products and services. The contribution of neural networks would make it possible for companies to engage customers and employees at an equal level. Customers would become off-roll employees and employees are anyway users also. Global navigation systems are becoming more and more intelligent to locate, track and find a thing or person. In future it won't be necessary to tag items with RFID (say) the advanced global tracking systems can find any man-made articles or resources or matter from satellite imagery. The use of drones and flying grasshopper cameras can go to any remote corner of the world and capture the essence of earth in natural resources, human habitation, or flora-fauna. Businesses can then exploit the presence of any product-related raw material or skilled resources. This is true especially of the present shift towards natural and herbal products for our consumption. All durables and fast moving goods like shampoo, cookies, oils, personal care products, food items including noodles are moving towards the use of herbs, grains, plant extracts, and seeds. Businesses would increasingly shift to the use of these ingredients in 100% totality. Today energy drinks and food nutraceutical are gaining importance because they are power-packed capsules. The trend will take crests and troughs to find optimum demand-supply with natural ingredients. This is a combination of total purity on one side and high modernity on the other end. Our sustenance would be based on natural-substance oriented businesses. Our progress would *be based on hi-technology oriented businesses. Thus the total business would be conducted on the lines of green business to preserve the natural sustenance and uplift the technology. Technology would be the pin-point for all business advancement. No technology can advance the business per se but can catalyse all the business activities to the optimal levels. We, as buyers, do not invest in technology but the quality and technical panache that appear in the products or services backed by such advanced technologies. Modern technological equipment like surgical or robotics can create wonders because of precision and skilfulness. Industry effectiveness and efficiency increase with the help of technology alone. Buyers don't buy technology but unconsciously appreciate technical applications. The objective of technology is not to make usage technical too. Usage should be simple but functioning should be complex. The* technological products should be able to incorporate complex functions but when they come in to the hands of a user they should be auto-usable. Minimum instructions and automatic guidance should come out of the shape and make of the product. Green and clean technologies with least carbon prints would be the next century's machines. No carbon prints is yet a dreamer but may come out true in due course with the help of whiz kids who become into technological geniuses. The balance between technology and its output on the surroundings would be created with the help of new compounds that achieve radical objectives without contaminating the environment. There would be no issue of chloro-fluoro-carbons nor the carbon monoxide nor the lethal output gases or metals on the row. The future rows would be totally oriented towards making business excellence out of better and better technologies than each day. Technologies would be *markers on businesses visible on products, promotions or operations. Any company lacking in appropriate technology cannot compete with the best and would have to nest with the weak ones giving rest to the success. The proponent of success in business would be technology in the future world but technology that is completely flexible in adaptation and usage. The two ends of application and usage would be nicely bridged. Every new technology would have to upgrade itself before being applied to products. Every product would have to live itself before being used by the consumer. Products would be auto-tested without the manual interference and the maintenance feature would also include auto-testing every brief interval. The products would elevate themselves based on technological assay. The labs would roll out products with multiple features and operative capabilities which would slowly unfold with the customers. Most of the times, the driver is not aware when auto-gear cars change gears but speeds. We are aware of the different features of products but never of how the internal operations take place. One more level of operations would include the unwrapping of different memory levels of products to use different technical components for improving operations of the products with time. Auto-intelligence of products to change according to user habits is the key driver of tomorrow's business. Food products are viable to be self-stocking and preserving by emissions of natural preservatives rather than depending on refrigerator storage or locker containers. Packaging would also be a new feature of products. Businesses today handle exclusively the packaging function alone. The wrappers or containers or boxes are treated with human-friendly substances. The future packaging would include storage substances so that the products increase in shelf-life, storage-period and freshness.*

Any product, whether food or non-food, of tomorrow

would be extremely user-friendly in – usage, health,

hygiene, storage and disposal.

All businesses would work towards conserving energy in all forms- renewable and non-renewable in the coming centuries. We don't know how much water will be left in the nature for us to drink but developing techniques to convert salt-water and rain water into useable drinkable water is one technological miracle foreseen in the future. Business ideas would be more inclined towards overall environmental up gradation because human efforts to live in luxury would have already depleted most of the natural resources. Social responsibility in corporate would thus be functioned towards community benefits via products and services. Recycled paper, organic food, dispose-as-per-use, low carbon, low pollution, low waste would all be visible in the business offerings of all companies in the next century. The life of corporates and citizens would be alike.

Every user of any business service or product would be termed as corporate citizen. A corporate citizen is thus a user or business exponent. Companies would model their businesses as per user demand. To satisfy a corporate citizen is to add to the global account of business presence. A corporate citizen would get all products and services based on the level of usage rather than the capability to pay. The more the usage the more is the growth of business. Companies would be responsible more towards the growth of corporate citizens than the business. The whole business world would function more as a banking firm than itself. A bank not only stores and secures our money but also provides money in times of need, with a guarantee or without any. Business of next century is going to take similar shape with the corporates aiming to provide safety to customers' emotions and expectations. In return they would gain the customer trust that is difficult to neither sell nor buy. The business growth is a growth of the direct users in next century. Today growth is rise in number of employees, offices, etc. Business need not be self-obsessive or narcissist. A business is more successful if it cares more for its customers. Take any company or entity in the whole business history and all successful companies are so because of their customers' trust in them. Earlier it used to take hundreds of years or at least decades to form trust. Customer and employee trust are equally important for a company's success. Future business is going to create trust more than anything else within its customers and employees. Technology is pre-defined. Preferences are known. Communication is transparent. Now what is left is trust to nurture and enhance. The involvement of customers and employees is so much more than every past that trust alone can create opportunities, innovation and growth for a business. Each century would see increasing importance of trust as a driver of success. Corporates would develop business individuality backed by robotics and technology, only with the help of trust. Kotler, Porter and Prahalad have all indicated trust as the most important factor in market, strategy and customer. Kotler has repeatedly harped on trust as deciding factor where customer trust is the bridge between companies and markets. Porter has discussed the importance of trust whether between nations, competitors or customers as a strategic success. Prahalad has time and again directly stressed upon trust to win the customers from all ends – lowest to highest end of spending spectrum, for ensuring business success. Trust is going to take a shift from being behavioural to strategic importance in business in the coming century.

Every strategy would be driven by future business trends rather than goals alone in the next century. Rather, the goal achievement would become a pre-requisite for business evolution. Technological and business trends would determine the business strategy of each corporation. The future and past trends would draw the present scenario for each business. The current business clusters would evolve into business success rather than company success. Each business success in the coming centuries would belong to a conglomerate of companies rather than a single one. Each supplier, manufacturer, distributor, guarantor, financing institution, buyer would determine their group's success and no single entity would be a winner or leader in the next century. The groups or clusters would become known identities in the market may be coined by a name or number. This is not to stay that there would be again portfolios or baskets of companies as in the stock bourses that would be formed as clusters. Rather, the winning group of different stakeholder conglomerates would be formed out of synergies that drive towards one another. The business accessibility of each entity in a given industry, strengths of each entity, expertise in their domain, cross-dependence on related industries, capabilities and technologies would bring together the different sets of companies to make an emerging, winning or leading business. Even advertisers and promoters can join the league in becoming a part of winning establishment. A shoe business would not be a leader by the name of Nike or Adidas or may be (what's in a name?). The business would become leader as a group of Nike, Adidas, Ogilvy, Radisson, Prada, et al. The winners in each sector or a combination of leaders-players can make business success. The next century's business success would need groups or teams because business is not going to be so simple. It would be drastically fast and dramatically swift. The entire product or service life cycles would be reduced to minuscule when brought down to execution. They would be lasting only a few seconds or less than that. The whole chain from manufacturing to final sale including payment would be carried out at such a finely executed pace with a number of players in the game hitherto unknown to business-kind. Mankind would become a reopener in the hands of technology. The inputs from buyers also would be minimal. The inputs would follow pull mechanism. The Blu-ray kiosks would gauge the basic needs of buyers like size, dimensions, past-purchase trends etc. to deduce the current purchase needs. Exotic options like add-ons, frills etc. would take a few more seconds. Payments and all would be seamless and not require any approvals. If the product is shipped or moved from the purchase stalls out of the store it is deemed to be a purchase. The bank or card details of buyers would be used against deductions, balances etc. Packaging would in a sense lose its appeal as compared to today. The buyer would take the product and on her own unless it is shipped to address. The product would not be packaged unless required by its functionality or storage needs. Thus the entire business cycle would be totally customized to each buyer's needs and hence each cycle would take seconds to complete from end-to-end to execute millions and zillions of business cycles for multitudes of customers. Logically, the internet revolution would convert into business revolution, thus technology taking the entire business under its wrap. Branding and labelling would also thus become a single sticker or stamp and not multiple ones each for one participant of business. The business group logo would suffice the representation of all companies on a product or article. Our own laptops would come with a sizeable cubicle or slot to transmit articles. Thus the internet revolution would become a revolution of things or technology that can transmit things along with data. The creation of products would be automated to such an extent that a pen could be created using formula of Parker, raw material of Rolex and transported through Japan's jet or bullet airway, roadway or internet-way. A new channel of distribution would be developed which can revolutionize the entire way of business in the next century. Products and services, whether small or large, would find a way of transfer from _____ to buyer's point. The blank is to indicate that the source may not be even relevant in the next century. The items may be manufactured at the buyer's point itself. Whoa, how's that? The user's end would see the entire business cycle before getting the product. This is the revolution of things where the raw material is present in every user's premise, process is software and output can be generated at the buyer or user or customer's premise. The advancement of technology would make it possible beyond the realms of imagination. The product world itself could transform in such a way that business would be conducted across net and not boundaries. The removal of distances between various process points in a production cycle or distribution cycle can expedite the business by hundred times. This is going to happen in future… The middlemen would anyway be eliminated but the key point to be noted is the increase in value-addition by many times as compared to today. Every buyer gets what she needs. Thus optimization is to the optimal levels possible. The pricing would be instantly set based on the single purchase. Decimation or not, the buyers would choose their price and product strategy. Profits would be distributed seamlessly among different stakeholders in a business. Stakeholders are in different sectors but contribute to a single buyer's success. Buyer's success in products is business success in industry. The more the number of buyer successes, the better the chances of the businesses being innovative for future sustenance. Margins would be propagated by buyers themselves or can be created by technologies based on the depreciation cycles, business financial status and product benchmarks in the market. Neither monopoly can be created nor can cartel form because technology would rule the market. The even game rules would be set by technology that would auto-evolve itself. What is going to gain importance is the output. What is the buyer getting? How is the buyer getting? The extent of customer delight is personalized. Each customer's delight is individual and may not be the other customer's. What is the business doing? How can the business be improved? The business excellence would be the key question rather than leadership or competition. Excellence would again be based on individual firm's goals and market expectations. The next century's buzzword would be technology but backed by Big B – buyer. Technology would flow between customers-distributors, dealers-packagers, packagers-assemblers, assemblers-manufacturers and manufacturers-procurers. Only the pace is going to be dotted. The invisible hand of technology would be a paradox for every business. How is the presence of technology improving the business? What is the contribution of technology to customers in present and future? No customer would understand the technology fully-well but would use it forever.

Technology cannot always be depended upon or blamed for any business failures. Ultimately technology is driven by innovation and innovation is driven by research. Research is driven by grinding others' ideas, weighing current scenario, generating new solutions. All these are possible by finding current problems. Every century comes with its own set of problems. Competitive laws, regulations, global scenarios, investment laggards, economic slowdown, inflating prices, volatile interest rates etc. are some of the common problems. New times would bring in new problems like technology complications, up-gradation balance, version uniformity, innovation barriers, and adoption inertia. There would be less and less of boundary or global divergence problems but more of convergence problems. The differences would be bridged but a commonality problem would emerge in the next century business. The nations would compete not to remove their cultural differences, governance loopholes, currency barriers but to create excellence in innovation and adoption. A nation like South Africa may itself fast enough to bridge the natural resources gap and also the regulations barrier to create a safe ground for business but may become a common ground for all innovation to be dumped in. It then has to decide how to balance the levels of innovation to come up with a nurturing platform for a common innovation. The common innovation between developing and developed nations would then have to be differentiated to suit different customer segment needs rather than country technology needs. The commonality between nations and convergence of technologies would create a need to manage customer differences. The differences may be in the same region or separate ones. The regions would thus start reconciling customer needs to again run up themselves towards a common technology graph. Once the customer level is uniform the differences would emerge at the national level again that have to be balanced. The crests and toughs would thus run among nations and individuals rather than the companies in the next era business. The challenge is to reconcile differences and create a differentiator to make the business common but innovation uncommon among nations.

Labs would have to be managed to create different innovation parameters so as to make the same technology capable of being run in different forms for the user needs. Imagine a world where Windows OS becomes the base for all computers, mobiles, microwaves, cars and stores. I am hinting at such a convergence. Next, imagine a world where the innovation on OS platform can be created in different forms to suit school learning needs, office communication needs, house maintenance needs and virtual shopping needs. The commonality is created out of the differences. At the same time, new differences emerge from the on-going innovation.

Chapter 7

New Business Dimensions – Avatar

How is leadership going to manage all these changes? This is a pertinent question especially in the light of reduced need for manpower in the coming century. Leadership would be redefined to function at different cluster levels and not at an individual company level. Each firm would be founded on strong principles by its leaders but their recognition would be based on the combined business success of all the value-chain participants. As discussed above, a single firm's success would no more be a success tomorrow. For a single business to be recognized as successful in the market, all its business stakeholders and participants in the entire value-chain have to emerge successful. Hence the leadership roles is going to be even more complex than today. Leaders have to participate at vertical success of firm's operations and contribute to horizontal success of all other participants in the business. Hence leaders of all conglomerates have to come together to bring about success based on strategies, finances, marketing, collaboration, competition, services, products, brands, skill, technologies etc. The methods of leadership management would vary from motivation, behavioural, coaching, mentoring, role-modelling, appraisal-based, goal-formation, inspirational, team-based, managerial, flexible and x-y-z. These are all book-based but the key ingredient of next gen leader is followership. The leader is going to be noticed only by being in the last of the league. A leader who fights for the front row is going to be seen last. Leaders would be following others to take note of weaknesses that they would in turn cover to boost the entire pace of the league. Gone are the days when a leader would vanish with the keys of secret success and business followers would search, imitate and copy to recognize leader in her. The new leader is going to forego the entire limelight, so to say, and dedicate all skills towards making leaders of others. Only those who make or create leaders can themselves be recognized as ones. In converting the entire business value chain into a success, it takes all leadership skills and hence such mentors would be capable of becoming leaders. Business also needs such skills in its leaders for next century. Each decade would see emergence of new types of leaders specializing in one skill but still capable of handling all others. The groups of all such leaders would become a winning business leadership formula for next century. Technology and leadership would become the successful combination in business. It needs efficient and ethical leadership to manage the ultra-tech business evolution. Innovation is always vulnerable to hackers and brokers. Thieves are always on the look-out for taking business loopholes into a never-ending crisis. Leaders of tomorrow must be capable of predicting, avoiding, managing such scenarios of crisis. Man-made, nature-made, a combination of both- all are possible business debacles to be managed by leaders. Geeks can but hackers need some strict sticks to be controlled. Leadership hence cannot be ignored in the future business.

Leaders would manage investments, guide innovation, accord sales, create brands, and resolve value-chain issues, train value-chain partners, and make new leaders. The concept of blue-ocean leadership would emerge to make leaders out of non-leaders. It is easier to make 100% non-leaders into complete leaders than to make a slow-growing leader into a complete leader. The carrot-and-stick would still hold true in the advanced technology era because business runs on money and stick is necessary to prevent the misuse of money. Showmanship and showbiz leadership days are gone when leaders used to claim all carrots for themselves and leave sticks for others. True leadership is capable of converting non-skilled into skilled, followers into leaders, non-achievers to goal-seekers, inert into agile, mediocre into excellent, losses into profits and imitators into innovators.

Innovation is not restricted to leadership or technology. Any new idea can be innovated, and made into a product or service using a new framework, a new technology and a new service by anybody high or low in organizational echelons. Business can be evolved along multiple dimensions. The sectorial specialization, market leadership, organizational growth, learning, strategy, and technology are the various dimensions of business. Innovation can occur at any of the heights. The sectorial specialism is the mastering of expertise and garnering of special skills relevant to the industry. It is possible with the help of hiring, training and grooming personnel, in different fields. Innovation can be pursued by developing a new skill or lab with the best resources. There is more to it for future business. Sector focus and specialization are glocal factors in any business. The focus should be local and expertise should be global. Innovation output is in the form of new products, services, packaging, usage methods, accessories or technology. The expertise can be developed to coincide with other industries or create dependence on other sub-sectors. Businesses take their own time to become industry experts but this dimension is not an option. Every business has to master itself to compete with others in the next century. Increasing competition means increasing specialization and vice versa. Hence the pre-requisite is now a competitive factor. Though there are lot of other players, the company has to find its own way of business to sustain in future. Mastery of skills, operations, procedures, routines, deadlines, budgeting, scoping, capacities, planning, resources, allocations, all come through trained personnel, expert consultants, skilled technicians, wise managers, alert supervisors, agile leadership, latest equipment, new production techniques, new manufacturing formulae, upgraded technologies and years of experience. When a business starts it adopts that industry standard and works towards attaining proficiency in the entire life-cycle of products or services offered by that company. As it grows, it standardizes some of those operational processes and attains expertise in the process. As it matures, it evolves its own niche and specialization. At this juncture, if the firm can reinvent some of its procedures to give extraordinary benefit of scale and scope then the company is said to reach a phase of ever-increasing growth as against the saturation stage hitherto known in industry evolution. Future business is going to evolve in a continuous growth with the help of innovation. The industry cycle would see large-scale specializations leading to replacement of saturation phase with innovation phase. The readiness and growth of a firm can be put on a rolling success cycle if it adopts innovation with specialization. Next century business can enhance specialization of sector by innovating HR processes, operational procedures, policies, routines, career growth, organizational development methods, motivational techniques, production techniques, engineering cycles, core products, service mechanisms, customer relationship management, product formulae, manufacturing methods and employee efficiency. Some companies solely depend upon employee skills and effectiveness. However, this is risky because of attrition. Specialization can be created in technology or policies rather than workforce. Manpower can also be specialized and retained by adopting employee-friendly policies. Employees can be motivated and made to be special assets of a company. Whatever specialization is achieved must be documented and circulated among all employees of the firm. Communication or lapse can make or break the specialization. Innovation on specialization is possible by giving complete freedom to employees to come up with new ideas and techniques. Managers should be allowed decision-making powers. Town-halls, seminars, open-houses, freestanding meetings, and debates should be conducted among employees and management teams to encourage innovation. A German technique may be best suited to the company but it may be following a Japanese method. In such cases, knowledgeable employees must be invited to judge the efficacy of methods and advocate the best. The organizational parlance must be adaptive to the new specializations emerging in the market. It is not much needed to compete in order to specialize. Specialization needs complete internal focus on firm's methods and can be made by involving the employees deeply in the organizational methods. The more the employees are involved in the firm's evolution, the quicker the specialization can be made. Coca Cola made the secret formula that is still locked in its company safe locker. The contributors are its employees whose trust it won in order to keep it specialized. Maggi made a secret formula for its noodles but couldn't keep away its key employees from leaving. The formula got diluted in many forms after being rolled out in the market by different firms. The latest rut of unhealthy levels of ingredients has challenged the mission of Nestle as a nurturer of kids. Coca Cola has innovated scores of products in each country with tremendous success because its specialization radar is intact. Maggi has created multiple products but on a weak specialization dashboard that has attracted devious controversies and variant products merely provided as a market offering. Companies that show themselves with specialization can better use market research feedback than the ones not with specialization as it creates a credibility for the firm with the old and new customers. Customers are important in getting product needs but how credible are you as a firm to extract that information from customers? Why should customers trust a firm if its employees don't? There should be trust between employees and the leadership for specialization to flourish in a firm. The senior management, board, middle management, lower-rung employees, consultants, vendors and clients are all part of the employee chain within an organization. Different groups interact with one another after incorporating trust within each other to get strategies, policies, rules, charters set. The market gets a tang of the same trust that is ripe within a firm. Next, market builds upon the trust if the firm specialization is worth the recognition or enough effort is expended. Customers or end-users give the final word on trust. They create the trust for firm's products thus giving a seal on the specialization and market response. It takes time to build that trust and it is not a one day's job, which no technology can also help with even in next century's business. However the overall business environment would be favourable and innovative to create a trust among all business stakeholders.

Market leadership can be attained with the help of operation excellence, setting benchmark, and conquering revenues.

Innovation is possible by working on higher benchmarks each time and optimizing the improvements on best practices. Organizational growth occurs by increasing volumes, sales, manpower, investments, expansion, market size, customer base, technologies, research, resources and capabilities. Innovation here implies creating combinations of resources and customers to get maximum return and value-addition. The output of innovation can be patents, blue-ocean strategies or a new technology invention. Organizational learning is a dimension that is inherent within every business and defines the progress of every firm in the industry. It helps in organizational development and involves skill-experience consolidation with the advantage of dynamic knowledge portals. Innovation means the process of learning to be revamped and merged with organizational planning. Market leaders are those that innovate for others to follow or copy or imitate. Some market leaders tend to be aggressive in their strategies but such a practice makes leadership short-lived and the strategy hollow. Business leaders excel at what they do, how they do and when they do. Markets always shred towards unhealthy competition but welcome pie-sharing among healthy leaders. Market leadership creates brand leadership for customer-oriented products or solutions. The share price escalates and vying for stock ownership encourages a spirit of competition among all participants in a business thus making it a fight for market leadership based on superiority rather than dominance. Some companies suffer from complex of technological or other superiority but such a high esteem must be backed by customer orientation in order to win the profits. Market leadership is not denoted by profits alone but by customer loyalty, employee retention, investor confidence and trading activity. Employees are internal but their skills are precious in market. Customers are external but their say is valuable to the market. Investors are profit-savvy but their buy-sell-hold decisions are drivers of the market direction. Trading is volatile but the bustle keeps the feedback, changes, and finances flowing in the economy. Increasing customer bases, expanding widely and locally, rising stock numbers, nurturing employee skills-scope-levels, snowballing products and services list, offering price-discount-freebies, balancing competitor forces with internal tactics and updating technologies with innovation are all ways of achieving market leadership. The ways are not sure-shot but necessary to gain the share. Be a leader but be innovative leader. Innovative leaders create spaces for others to become leaders as well as innovators thus creating a self-challenging space. They keep raising their own benchmarks and often excel them easier than others who compete aggressively to lose out in wars. Innovation inspires others to think forward. It is better than blame-games and business wars. Nit-pricking or fault-finding businesses hardly survive the market turbulences. Competitive wars are not short-cuts for becoming leaders as most companies think. Coke-Pepsi war was more of market need then than market reaction. The evolution was such that the war was inevitable. These days' business firms enter into artificial wars only to get noticed in the market. These are called pathetic strategies. Future would curtail all such pathetic or bad strategies. They are unproductive strategies as the result is more trial-and-error and chance than sure-shot. Innovation should be in the direction of unravelling new ways for leadership and not beating other's ways. Corporate social responsibility is also a part of the market leadership. Once the company gains a considerable share, it must distribute some of its impact to the needy. It need not give profits to poor but take up social projects to lend properties, donate articles, build schools, sponsor village adoption and reduce pollution. Though it is an extended form of market leadership, yet, it has often been seen that responsible companies are treated with a positive light by market and customers. Innovative firms can design their own innovative leadership programs to help business and community at a time. Market leaders create balance between corporate and social efforts. Business is defined as monetarily profitable on-going entity. Leaders always do something extra. This extra is CSR. Future is going to immensely involve CSR within business goals in such an intrinsic way that business would give 50% focus to customers and 50% to community in the next century. The social needs would also transform themselves from current needs for schools, water, roads etc. to those for technological advancements of backward or developing regions, standardizing gadget use among different societal hierarchies.

Strategy is a unique dimension of organization evolution which is inclusive of planning, innovation and goal achievement. The innovation is in terms of execution methodologies, goal-sequencing and milestone attainment. The decision management can be innovated to attain optimal strategies within a time period. Strategy can be managed at different situations from different locations by tying up goals with tasks. Global business seeks strategies on an on-going basis to combine rational skills with non-rational, tangible with intangible, assets with liabilities and failure with success. Rational skills are the knowledge frameworks and soft-skills like communication. Non-rational skills are the gut feelings that often go with customer preferences. Tangible results in terms of revenues, share price, market share, growth figures, returns and profits have to be managed along with non-tangible results like knowledge, learning, best practices, brand value, global recognition and business impact. Business impact involves passion of stakeholders, dedication of employees, and respect for customers. The affection for business and strategic orientation together can understand and pull in customers or investors from various fronts. All assets and no liabilities mean that the business is playing too safe and risk-averse. It also indicates that the company is not tapping in all available resources to grow itself. Strategic learning is necessary for implementing future strategies based on a failure or success of all business stories. The market presents different genres of strategies like growth, investment, expansion, human resource, supply-chain, financial, market, operations, leadership, branding, packaging, distribution, storage etc. The list can be as long as the business itself. Strategy is a dimension that is timeless and priceless. Though strategy is valued highly by consulting firms, the corporates can carve out their own strategies by giving a chunk of time and effort of old or new employees. Here's a small recipe for successful business strategy formulation. Hire 80% new strategy experts and reuse 20% top slot exclusively for strategy formulation. As a firm, keep strategy separate from all other activities or meetings. First, implement and then start mixing with as-is. Next, allocate double the fees that you would otherwise pay to a top consulting firm. Seriously, build up the funds like you would for an outside consultant. You would notice that more than 80% would be unutilized but still keep out the fund. Also don't start getting greedy of saving 80%. Just focus on strategy. Infuse the need for strategy in each meeting. Schedule at least one daily meeting as you do any other task like production or customer call daily. Remember that now strategy is an additional role and responsibility of your firm. Or, to make it simple, strategy is a new product and you are its vendor-client. Keep drawing charts, creating presentations, drafting documents and crunching numbers on excel sheets. Pull out new ideas, brainstorm with young and experienced. Make a master-plan with the top stakeholders [say, increase revenues by 50% by next year and become No.2 player in market]. Draw subsequent plans with each department [number of product, target customers, pricing etc.]. Make plans for sustainability [loyalty schemes, offers, memberships etc.]. Prepare a task force of key 20 or 30 members for Strategy team. Roll out action plans and task list on a task force. Like a project management plan, indicate budget, resources, milestones, status updates, revisions, scope, targets and stakeholders. Plan top management meetings at least once a week. Monitor the success and declare the strategy to the market and wait for the feedback. Reward all the teams involved in strategy formulation and implementation especially the heads. Leaders and teams need to be rewarded equally for business success to be sustainable and penetrate into future planning. Now, share the strategy among all departments and the lessons-finding of the entire journey. Prepare a knowledge base and follow the case studies of failures and successes in the market. A real strategy is the one that is adaptable to market changes and achievable in company books. Innovate the frameworks and create new benchmarks, use new technologies and methodologies to implement old robust strategies. Don't go by the book or rote but by situation or business scenario. Copy as much as you can follow and not blindly including failure steps of other's strategies.

Technology is a business dimension of differentiation and inclusion for tomorrow's world. Innovation is all in here. It can be a different mode, device or procedure that can create a new technology. All dimensions put together, must encourage innovation in such a way that all questions of a given time are addressed, all business needs are accommodated, all customer requirements are included and all opportunities are tapped. The dimensions are themselves never fully explored or exploited by companies. Technologies are increasing in versions, grades, forms and levels. This is only going to get more complex in the future. Often companies compromise on quality because of expense constraints. They go for used equipment, or low-grade machinery or out-dated versions of technology. However, the latest technologies should be adopted for best results. The cost of investment is high but duration for yields is same for both low and high grade technology. The transition would be easier as technology becomes complex and better if a company is already at a newer version. Market is on a growth track as against companies that are on volatile tracks. Market is going to see newer technologies and developments with time. Companies can grow or sink with time. Hence it is better to acquire technologies as per market benchmarks rather than internal company conveniences. Conveniences prop up according to managerial preferences, risk appetites, financing schemes, dealer recommendations and competitors. It is better to place decisions against competitors and market to create optimal capabilities than against internal stakeholder choices to end-up with out-dated mechanisms. Technology innovation is another area where a company must concentrate after acquiring reasonably adequate capabilities. A company must create a R&D team and lab for technology advancement. The geeks and scientists should get motivation and rewards for innovating along the upcoming technology trends and acquire as many patents as possible. The benefits are many. First, the firm itself would be capable in all ways if it owns the advanced technology along with the creators of that. Second, the market would set benchmarks against the focal firm's capabilities thus making it a leader. Third, the royalties of use by others generates revenues and competitive foothold in the market. Fourth, it is easy to forecast future and work along new requirements thus having a better access to future customers and technologies. Fifth, technology is inclined towards automation, robotics and artificial intelligence. All research should take place in this direction to work along improving future scope, business excellence and process automation.

Business scenarios should indicate the approach of firms in the future. There are both constant and variable business scenarios.

1. Organizational Agility – is a constant business scenario where lack of agility means inertia into which firms would not slip into to remain competitive. Market changes must be monitored constantly, competitors must be observed and relevant strategic action should be taken to overcome the situation.

2. Organizational Learning – is a constant business scenario where a firm keeps learning from its failures and successes. The tacit and expressible learning comes from employees, case studies, competitors, market and innovation.

3. Technology – is a variable business scenario where firm should go on updating itself according to the latest trends. Technical knowledge is necessary to understand and use technology and to further convert into end-customer usable products.

4. Resources – is a constant business scenario that needs men, material, money in some or the other project as long as business is in existence.

5. Restructuring – is a variable business scenario as it occurs once in decades to handle market changes and internal reorganizations. The balance between internal and external change has to be maintained by restructuring the design, structure, and hierarchy, business offering portfolio, operations and subsidiaries.

6. Co-alienation – is a variable business scenario where companies sometimes collaborate, and compete at other times. They cooperate in some scenarios and operate in confidentiality in scenarios of research and innovation.

As discussed above, constant and variable business scenarios are broad categories. Other scenarios are fluctuating, volatile, predictable, unique, repetitive, opportunistic (identifies problems), random, and oceanistic (identifies opportunities). Fluctuating scenarios occur when market is indeterminate about a need or requirement of end-user. Volatile conditions are not new, market is always volatile. Predictable scenarios occur when forecasts and simulations help know future goals and conditions of markets. Unique scenarios occur when unknown or unseen market events unfold into a unique opportunity or challenge. Repetitive business scenarios occur because of success replication, imitation or sequels of regulations. Opportunistic scenarios leave out problems created by competitors for industry leaders. They may arise out of innovation or price-wars. Oceanistic scenarios allow players to pick up opportunities from unknown or under-exploited areas. Random scenarios are driven by competitive acts or gut-feel strategies. They are risky and dramatic business scenes.

All business scenarios must be responded to by keeping in mind the following elements –

Technology + Skills + Capabilities

+

Time [of entry, exit, execution]

+

Accuracy and precision of strategies

+

Goals (estimates)

+

Actuals

+

Resources

It is a combination of all above ingredients to prepare for the recipe of business scenario management in the future generations business. Disaster management is possible by handling each business scenario with an appropriate mix of above. In some cases, resources assume utmost importance, in others, technology or entry-exit strategies may be more important than others. It is up to the top management to assess each business scenario and prescribe a resolution mix to the middle management for implementation.

Business success comes based on the excellence in internal growth, competition, static or dynamic achievements. The dependence on leadership suggests in most research reports that women should be in majority in any firm to succeed because they bring in soft skills, excel in unequal pay situations and are more adaptive of business environment. The personal-professional balance that they carry into the workplace ethics reflect in business success. Management should recommend more women for promotions, pay-hike and incentives. It should be achieved gradually. The pay between male and female employees has never been uniform in most of the firms. The gap needs to be bridged to encourage a healthy women workforce. More options of work-from-home and remote offices should be provided. Remote offices are those that are fully run and managed by women employees. They are situated away from the local bustles or downtowns and more in residential towns. The intuitive sense of women can also help predict various business scenarios and act upon in advance of competitors. The business sixth sense comes from its women employees in junior, middle and top management. An ideal combination is to have 50% women in junior ranks, 40% in middle tiers and 70% in top management. Leaders are better-off in guiding the company through times of crisis and success with equal passion if they are women than if men. The role of women in business should be emphasized because it is going to get more and more important in the coming times. The balance is shifting in similar ways on the home front. In personal life, men are contributing to wives' tasks. Household and kids are shared equally by men and women. The outside work – office, shopping and bills are also shared in equal ways. Where husband and wife work in the same office, they manage different shifts at home and work. Sometimes, they come in early and leave by afternoon to spend time with kids. When they work in different places, women are equally taking charge of family. Professionally, women need to undergo an image change when women have been known for homemakers or caretakers. The next century woman would be known for her intelligence and agility rather than home and affection. Home is usually identified with a woman, mother or wife. Office is identified by man. The reverse is also true. The image is going through a shift but lot needs to change before next century business can be called business of equals. In the world of equals, why should business remain gender-centric? Women are more successful as leaders than men. There is no company or bank that went bankrupt under woman leadership. Still, women leaders have been fired, or transferred or demoted or blamed for failures. The perspective has to change. Companies can gain lot more because a woman creates an aura of her work wherever she does at home or office. A family is made by a woman. A business is also similarly raised by a woman where she gets a chance. Biotech is a good example of greatness achieved by business due to a woman. Yahoo is another example. Pepsi is a competitive example of a firm led by female CEO. This is not to say that men are not successful. Two successful participants are able to take business to heights faster than one. This is what I would like to indicate. Where men are able to handle physical tasks with excellence, women are able to handle mental pressures with excellence. Again, this does not mean that they can't do the others' tasks. Women are competing in physical excellence with men. Sports women and martial arts leading ladies are not uncommon achieving top laurels. If woman can reach top then she can as well manage physical activities in work or outside. Women ask questions and like to answer as well. Men ask questions but don't like to be questioned. There are cultural, gender-specific and behavioural differences between men and women that nobody can and should remove. However, biases based on false discrimination can ruin progress of economies and businesses. A woman is not stopped from taking up hard task like driving a truck, if she wants. Then why should she be stopped from leading a group of male scientists, if she wants? To a great extent, women are encouraged and motivated to work, but there's a still longer way. The gap increases as business complexity increases. Earlier, sales and marketing biases used to come up. Now technological and intellectual biases are coming up. Women face hurdles at workplace, and that is unacceptable by law and paper. However, the male counterparts are unable to accept the women interference in business progress. They are ready to lag down the pace than admit to women's ideas. A woman manager has to place in more effort for convincing the team than a male manager. The work is same, and the results are same. Hence such differences would vanish only with time. Of course, with virtual office spaces, it is hardly disclosed whether a man or woman is handling a task remotely. What matters is the output and quality. Video-conferences, teleconferences, seminars and meetings should be represented by both men and women in equal numbers. Companies should hire more women than men. The natural preferences of women also exist still. Women like to take breaks for raising kids or looking after families. Such natural causes should not be aggravated by companies not taking a tough stand of recruiting more female employees. Proper transportation and safety measures are adopted by various companies to encourage women staff. This would become even more rampant in tomorrow's business as women take initiative to lead success of firms. Research indicates that even today, business participation has more than 60% men all over the world. The ratio should become 1:1. It is bound to become more in the next century because women are keen on taking up additional responsibilities for same pay. Men demand more salaries and bonuses but research also points out that women never demand for hikes or perks. It is pertinent to point out that all-women and no men is not a risk-free proposition. Women come with their own problems and burdens. Men are more ego-centric. A balance is needed to ensure a sturdy workplace where men support women and create a healthy environment for work. A man does not have to think before stepping out but a woman has to take one or the other precaution for herself, if not for everybody. Physically, man is stronger than woman and can lift heavy things without worry. Exceptions arise but these are inherent strengths of man that carry him forth in the business world as well as otherwise. The path is converging as women tend to take more training for physical robustness and self-defence. Some companies are encouraging women athletes and sportspersons for internal growth. As more and more female members are getting educated, and creating their presence in every field, business also finds a time when all women would be fully equipped to handle any type of task in the future. The two crucial issues of safety and strength can be aided by robotic machines or sophisticated tracking gadgets. Business and management styles are changing with times and next century scholars are deemed to prepare better flexible models than today. The business models are prone to be flexible and adaptable so that the technological development can be continuous. No theory or practice can get stuck due to misalignment. Theory can improve along the lines of research that is more initiating than today. It should include future market trends along with other scholars' works. Moreover, real business scenarios cannot wait for others to forecast and prepare for. They would occur and recur as technology and skills develop. The gaps or opportunities would arise along with new practices. As discussed above, the leadership would be more encouraging and innovative. Hence the management style would be more learning-centric and free. There would be lot of innovation, research and ideation. The lifecycles would be so short that a new product developed during ideation would itself sell for a time before another new one comes up in the market. In other words, the utility of products and inventions would be increasing and instant. Even prototypes would be of some utility. Every product would be sold out. The prevalence of utility in small-to-big things is of immense importance in the coming years where no resource would be wasted. Every single penny would gain importance in investment and output. The customers would not compromise on the complete quality of products but neither would they ignore the small capabilities developed by companies. The maximum development is going to be in the healthcare. The sector is one that is gaining increasing importance in the coming decades. Technology and production would reach an automatic state of advancement. But healthcare is the area of emphasis because as companies work harder, they would have to redirect their research and innovation in the area of healthcare. The customers, diagnostics, remedies and medicine are heading towards a new journey. Where intellect and skill are reaching consummating heights the health and food are becoming issues and causes for concern. The quality and nutritional values are decreasing rapidly. Firstly the natural resources like fields and growing spaces are reducing. Next the use of artificial and genomes are giving rise to genetically modified food that loses natural ingredients in some form or the other. Then, the preferences themselves are changing to fast foods, energy foods and instant boosters. All these are creating health issues like cholesterol, diabetes, heart problems and skin problems. Milk is not pure; Vitamin D deficiency is creating bones and calcium problem. Vegetables are not fresh and nutritious enough to compensate for a day's nourishment. Fruits are not naturally ripe, nor good enough for day's diet. Staples are not naturally grown, and have not been able to provide the complete supply of proteins as earlier. Children eat more of pizzas and cakes. Adults diet on fries and cokes. Still, seniors are moving to oats and porridges. Refrigerated, frozen or pre-cooked meals are getting popular. Restaurants or home-delivery or drive-ins are seeing more crowds than kitchens at home. Home-cooked food is now a rarity and is going to become even more in the near future. Hence next century issues are major in terms of young diabetics or under-nourished. It is going to start quite early on in our lives. Children are more vulnerable to eye disease, and other adult ailments than today. Technology breakthroughs are predicted maximum in the healthcare industry. The diagnostics and medical equipment would be extra-modern and hi-frequency hi-tech machines would be needed to mend the humans. Our bodies would function more like machines than men, responding to pills and surgeries more than spinach and aerobics. The changing lifestyles are making us weak in all aspects. Hard work is the key to health but future would see hard work in terms of brain and less in body. The deliberate attempts to flex muscles or nerves would not be easy as our strength would not be adequate. The energy would be short-term and instant and instantaneous. The business houses would work more on innovation for health than for electronic gadgets. The shift of attention from FMCG to healthcare and insurance is of major relevance to the next century. What would doctors do with patients? They would treat more often online than in hospitals because the needs are going to be multiple for health. The injections and medicines would be administered by med-bots after diagnosis on patients. The word patient would lose its importance and usage because it would be universal.

More children would be treated rather than vaccinated. Today we prevent, tomorrow we cure. The environmental changes along with food intakes would change the health levels of all in the coming vestiges of burgers, pizzas and noodles. The advent of organics or multi-grains is not going to influence kid if the next century in anyway unless a radical innovation happens in the area to come up with delicious chocolates of organic fruit and yummy ice-creams made of millets. Labs are testing the produce and releasing results that the nutrients of today's yield are much less than the olden days'. Future forests don't seem to hold a better light than today. The diseases are also rampant and owners too. The onus is on us to take personal care of ourselves and each individual is apparently on a busy route for future to let go of all such worries. The resultant hit on health is going to gain online and virtual doctors' attention who would recommend customized diets daily for the users. The schedules and habits of next-gen-ers would keep the sector of healthcare on innovation path. New machines, tablets and medicines would be discovered and invented just as machines for gadget manufacturing. People would be keen on work and not health due to which deficiencies would surge and this would become a major business of the future. Medical consultants and personal nurses would be more rampant whether physically or online. Each person would need sophisticated diets tailored for oneself. New robotics inventions would happen to come up with solutions for critical ailments, including surgeries for artificial limbs and short-term genetic treatments where key genes would be modified to handle short-term life needs of human beings in the allocated life of 70-100 years. The future generations would further be affected by the prevalent trends and would need even more complex medical developments to handle their survival and existence. The new equipment and technologies should meet the product needs in the next century, which they will. In addition the new requirements would emerge for health needs which would be totally unexpected. Environmental pollution and rising temperatures would necessitate technology creation of apparatus and tablets to protect from the effects in addition to the falling nutrition levels. Management tactics would be driven more by new needs and emerging sectors than by trends or technological advancements.

Industries would be managed by demanding customers more than by stakeholders or investors. Customers would be so savvy of gaining edge on brands that companies' business would be driven by them instead of bosses. The changing organizational structures would also fill in the gaps of employee work-styles like Soho, remote-work, distance-office, or mobile-office trends. The hierarchies would be more or less flat structures and would be run on skills rather than on names. The brands would be created and managed by innovators and pay would be more commission-based than monthly salaries. Employees would work on profit-sharing mechanisms so that their stake in the firms increases and they become innovators. Renovating success is the next gen business mantra. Every success would be founded upon previous ones or imitated after other competitors'. This would occur due to the pace of the business that would be gasping. Frightening speeds of business decision and execution would put competitors under tremendous pressure to achieve big. Big would be the starting point followed by bigger and biggest in terms of employee count, sales volumes, revenue numbers, profit margins/ loss, product functionality, investments, budget allocations etc. Both profit and loss can be big. Therefore the players would either hit low or high in the very first game or launch. Where today's saturation point in industry evolution occurs, would begin the next world's business. Identity crisis would emerge among brands and companies alike because of the high stakes of multiple partners and fast business development cycles. The quick innovations would help in renovation of success by repeating, imitating, copying, following or revolutionizing other competitors' innovations. Defining the logistics of business every now and then would be a trend of future due to rapidly changing markets. It is true that market trends would be volatile in the future but on the whole they would be defined by the supply-chain links. An industry would be impacted by its supply-chain partners' preferences and capabilities along with customer demands. Customers are always on the verge of constantly questioning their own demands. Even supply chain of next century would be highly innovative. The simplest of the tasks would be innovated and thus success would be renovated. The complex tasks would be broken into simple ones before getting innovated. For example, the distribution cycle would be handled independent of the sales cycle. The process improvement would take live on business thus saving the time for testing or brainstorming.

The next century business in the profit sense would be so technologically advanced that the whole attention would shift to primary and secondary sectors. New social and economic initiatives would gain business importance in the next century. Companies would come up with latest technologies to handle issues of global importance. Government should start preparing in those lines and be more responsible towards the environment at large and country at hand. For example, the problem of storage and wastage in agricultural sector is not a small one. The food and grain storage, coupled with the twin problems of high price and wastage is a serious concern for the coming ages if left unresolved. Technologies should be procured by the government; projects should be tendered to business houses for building silos or storage facilities to facilitate accessibility of food to all at the right price. This is not only a problem in India but also in many countries. The percentages of wastage differ but exist in all parts of the world for the simple reason that produce is not rationed appropriately for masses but distributed to aggregators, traders, processors and manufacturers for inputs or end-products supply at various locations. Warehouses and silos have as much granaries as built by owners and sought by buyers/ sellers. There is still a lot left unused, or wasted or sold in distress at any place in the beginning, middle or end of the value-chain whether at supplier-end or processor-side or buyer-end. The complete profitable sale is said to occur when the entire produce can be sold at a standard price and that too to all needy (rich and poor) without wasting a single morsel. This is a big challenge for the next century business but not difficult to resolve. The logistics have to be worked online based on access-storage-requirement matrix. Where is the produce available? Where is it needed? How can a common storage be built for buyer and seller? How can it be disposed of for further sale or processing? How can the intermediaries interact with one another to wrestle between the prices to keep them at uniform rate? How can government ensure real-time tracking of all stocks moving from field –farmer - producer – storage – supplier – processor – intermediary – buyer – storage – distributor – dealer – stores – consumer? The next century technology would and should facilitate tracing each grain from farmer to fork. It would not only help the farmers and manufacturers and consumers get the most out of the agriculture, but also grow the economy beyond industry. Though the primary sector is most important in every nation because of the direct connection of food with human existence, it is not gaining that pie in the economic growth as industry or service. Secondary and tertiary sectors are the most innovated and attended to. Agro-sector also now has to reach the technology excellence or rather business excellence. Agriculture including forestry is a business of life. Industry and service are both dependent on agriculture and vice versa. Industries compete for the raw material and products for FMCG in food, paper, wood, clothing etc. Industry recipients and sellers of all food products, apparel, textiles, housing, real-estate are completely dependent upon agricultural and forestry sector. Tertiary sector has outgrown the dependence of agriculture by including agriculture also as one of the services directly or indirectly. The whole food chain is dependent or commencing from agriculture. Once the secondary and tertiary sectors are defined and redefined along with innovation and technological revolution, then the whole business focus would shift back to primary sector. The opportunities and challenges would be handled in the agriculture and forestry areas by the next century business. There is tremendous scope in this sector specifically because it is a consistent need related directly to nature and natural resources. The nature's reservoir is endless but is not replenish able if not utilized wisely. Food business would be the buzzword of next century. Not in the form of consumption or mode of delivery but the source itself. The logistics, sustenance model, value-chain addition and value-add in agricultural industry are relevant for innovation models to be built for in the coming decades. Brazil, Argentina, USA, Australia, China, Canada, UK, Netherlands are all major agricultural importers and exporters. As disclosed by their Embassy leads of agro-sector, there are import-export related transactions happening on all sides that give rise to the storage needs and logistics improvements on an international front rather than on one region or national front. Thus improvement in the primary sector is going to be a business of future.

The purpose of business is to satisfy customers, now it is more of delighting customers, in future it would be to multiply customers. A customer who can network many more is more than a delighted one. The purpose of future business is to create a customer who can get many customers as meant by Shiv Singh when he said that the purpose of business is to create customer who can create customers. This is to start with a referral program, or loyalty program or rewards program, and a network program. To extend it further, the customer should also show loyalty towards the business. Customers are the most important but business should also be important to customers to the extent of marginalizing their shift to other business products in the markets and to further rope in others as customers. The others could be friends, family, peers or unknown participants in networks via social media. The social networks can manage customers but not create customers. Only existing customers can make more customers. This can be done through word-of-mouth, social media gadgets and apps, feedback or reviews, and meetings. Companies can create such multiplicand loyal customers not by rewards or gifts but by emotional aesthetics. The products would denote the intelligence of companies. The purchase trends would be rewarded with points. The discounts and offers can pull in non-customers. But a pinch of involvement in the entire business can excite a customer do some more for the concern out of sheer enthusiasm or inner urge and nothing more to do something for the company. The 'do-something-more' translates into tying up new customers who are loyal to the same extent because they come from inner circles of the existing customers. The new ones are those close to the heart of the customers. It is easier said than done. Both sides – company and customer – have to understand that business is more than buy-sell. At least it has to become so in the future if not today because that is the only direction of future business progress. Customers must not view business as a mechanical entity that can be seen in few products to be sold, bought, returned, exchanged or disposed of in the marketplace. Just as business should treat customer with priority, we also must display responsible attitude rather than one of concomitance with dominance. Customers should not ignore or denigrate the companies for small reasons or no reasons. Customers must understand that companies are also performing not for failure but which only happens due to improper resource allocation. A company fails not due to lack of resources but due to lack of proper allocation. Customers never excuse companies for any lacunae and are seen lashing them always for any fault or miss. It is ignored that those behind companies are also human and to err is human. Machines hardly err and that far so good. Customers are often seen picking on the weaknesses or defects in products and services of companies. Business flaws are more noticeable than strengths. This is not unacceptable because businesses are meant to be perfect entities in the market. Otherwise, each one of us can own and set up a loose business for meeting our household requirements. Hence business of future must strive towards excellence that can drive customers not only be satisfied and delighted but also be driven to excellence of recommendation. The recommendation should create many more customers who are hidden in the internal rungs of existing customers. These internal rungs rest the personal favourites of customers- parents, partners, best friends, uncles, aunts, bosses, mentors, disciples, students, et al who do not get the thumbs up unless there is lot more to the product than promised and expected. The sequence of excellence is from vision to plan to strategy to resources to technology. We have been reaching the end during the course of our journey towards excellence. Technology is not the dead-end, nor can we go back several times on the path. The next concurrent path for technology, customer and business is to align the customers with business in such a way that new customers are brought in by the existing customers. Customers' role is not one-off where there is one-time buy or loyalty enrolment for years but where there is passion or dedication of customers. How can busy customers concentrate on the companies? They can't. That is why we have to take it to the extreme. The extreme that the customers can do is to add more customers. Don't expect more or less. Let the customers do the talking. Groove interest into them for understanding the sentiments behind the business which won't come unless there are in fact some. Future business is going to see upheaval of behavioural and organizational sciences instead of economics or technology. Both these latter points would be explored to the fullest for enabling business move to the next state where the emphasis would be on raising emotional quotient of both employees and customers. The emotion creation does not stop at vision-mission but goes on into the manufacturing process, which is totally unknown to the customer to the sales process which is totally in the hands of customer. Customers hardly go to the website of company to read the mission or understand the operations behind their products. It is up to the companies to nurture the feelings in customers in favour of the products by working on the processes that take place behind the customers. Rather, it can be termed as ethics or integrity of highest levels that can be seen even in the unseen activities of business. The dedication or effort that goes into the activities of manufacturing should be felt in the final usage of the product. Some companies do that say in coffee manufacturing firms, the customers can feel the purity of coffee demonstrating the effort in collecting, cleaning, blending, mixing and making of coffee via aroma, taste and colour of the drink. The same 'feel' has to compete for all products and businesses of future. How a company is going to achieve that is a million-dollar question. It is critical for a business to focus all its employee effort onto the operations or products. Employees are human and digressed by multiple issues of life and career. Machines cannot ooze out emotions. Hence the only way is to train employees enjoy their work and earn solutions for even their personal problems out of their work ethic. Then no employee would shirk work. All employees would be pulled into their work mode and do the best which would make customers do their best for the business entity. As business would gain increasing technological application, it would gain increasing customer reorientation. In such cases customers would become co-partners or stock owners within the companies. Imagine customers who sell the company products in turn to others or facilitate the happening of same, for a decade, creating at least 2% of company revenues. No employee can also guarantee that she would contribute to at least 2% of total company sales. In such scenarios, customers are deemed shareholders because they are creating stakes and managing profits of the entity. The best business reward is to make such customers partners or board members by honouring them with equity partnership or shareholding. They in turn would gain so much credibility – both customers and company that each would work for the other's value-addition. Customers would create more avenues of loyal customer segments and companies would create more products of customer preference than the last time. Products and services would play into the customer sentiments favourably that would create more solutions and opportunities would be churned out endlessly. There is no better advocate of a company's product than one of its users. Taking more customers from customers is the best price for any company product and service.

The economic output is increasing each century that would only accelerate in the next century also. The global output is increasing by at least 4 times every century. The consumables are increasing, the options are plenty and the goods are several. The strenuous work that used to be in the last century is now simplified with the help of automatic tools and machines. Taking it a level higher with robotics, the number of hours that would be put in by the human beings in the next century would be lower than now. Employees would have to work much less than that today. They would be freed of daily tasks and burdened with important tasks like creating customer followership, product functionality, global communication tools or making advanced robots. All these would increase efficiency and usage of business. The operations would be efficient to give more offerings of products and services to be used by end-customers. The global plethora of products and goods would create a surplus in the market that would have to be measured against the input. The excess output would be enough to meet the global human existence needs of food, clothing, housing, including education and employment. Education would be promoted more online, mobile and virtual than face-face. Teachers could be robots, students would be human. Employers would be human, employees could be robots. The combination could be both robot-robot on the fronts to create a whole community of robots in colleges and offices. A college could be completely trained by and for robots. A workplace could be completely run by and for robots. The objective is to shoot up the output. The more the output, the more affordable and luxurious would be the lifestyle. Every lower segment of humanity can move up the levels due to the accessibility and affordability of output. If robots create and home-deliver cookies, what is the need for labor? The free employees can work on something else when they can work just an hour everyday instead of eight today. The value-addition would be highest under such circumstances where freed-up labor can focus better on personal growth and things of their interest. Dealing with robots involves defined activities like formulae. It is easier than dealing with human beings because no extra explanations or personal attitudes need to be addressed. It is more difficult to deal with robots than human beings because robots cannot understand the personal background behind demands or rationale behind extra demands. A customer may pursue extra warmth in getting convinced to buy a pack of cookies. The robot can give the latter but not the former. May be, the robots would be built with rays that can change our nerve movements and blood pressures to make us feel warm or angry. Hence the soft section would be missing with robots but nevertheless that can be compensated for by the human beings focusing on better solutions to humanity. Of course human beings should be more careful in prioritizing the functions like softness, logic or understanding, whether in themselves or robots. Hence the responsibility is nevertheless going to increase for future business along with the output, convenience and comfort. What we would get out of business next century is going to be much more than today, may be more than 6 times of the extant output. That's a different business world to handle and work with where we have more free time than work. The growth statistics would be more optimistic with higher CAGR, GDP rates, savings rates, investment rates, low inflation and better demand-supply balances. The returns would be better than today but have to be utilized wisely into better means each decade. The increased output in goods, services, accessories, does not mean increased access, hence better means of shipments or locations have to be devised with logistics to manage usage of the excess. The penalties on dumping or cross-border restrictions can be managed by balancing the output-need numbers across regions. The global trade barriers should be eliminated to transport the extra output to the areas in need of the same. There are lot of possibilities of economic growth due to augmented output in the global arena. The world would become a happy family of satisfied customers and companies that would lead the business among annals of success and prosperity. Let's hope that the business in next century would be more facilitating for both citizens and governments due to the amplified productivity. The yields would be higher than now and, the throughput would be higher than the past to make the past glowering than ever into which one would not want to step back. Today we feel that we live in golden times. Tomorrow we would be labelled as the most patient grandparents to have borne one of the darkest times of existence. Business would be that much overwhelmingly superb in the coming eras. This is a good indication. Business should improve than earlier with times. There should be something good in each century that can become better in the next. Everything should grow and so should output. The tools themselves may be used for new purposes after fulfilling the direct requirement of factory productivity. Technology and its applications are more and more efficient. Thus the mechanisms for increasing efficiency are also getting more efficient with the result that they can be utilized for multiple goalmouths in many different ways. When both the means and ends are efficient multiple objectives can be achieved. This gives efficient output more efficiently than earlier. Thus growth of the economy can be multi-dimensional. It creates more opportunities and avenues for development of individuals and corporates in the modern centuries. Some key business factors that would lose relevance in the next century are time management, planning and investment. It would be so innovative that time management would be the motivating factor behind every invention or business activity with in-built pace and speed. Hence time would no more be a concern of business. Planning would be swept by strategic sharpness of firms in the 2100s. Every strategy would be minutely crafted and still spontaneous the cause and effect being, no need for or no chance for planning. Investment would not be called for as in the given century because innovation would be everywhere and funding would be bounteous. The individuals and institutions would automate the investment process so well that a sure-shot return project would get invested the rest would be automatically chucked out of the global business. Thus only the successful ones would be invested and only those that get invested would be successful. There would be a world of difference in the next era business. One thing would sustain – success. All else would lose relevance in the world of business. Companies can manage themselves better and work on many things using the same pool pond of resources. Skills can be applied and procured from multiple pools of talent. To reiterate, there would be plenty of plenty. Plenty of business opportunities, plenty of business investors, plenty of time, plenty of resources, products, projects, sales, plenty of profits, would lead to plenty of success in the next century business. A business takes 100 years to form and succeed. Still a century seems to be a small time in the life of an entity. The coming aeons would classify themselves as shelf life of business for the simple reason that every business would be a success or at least near success with strictest of the competitors gasping their innovations for reaching the best of utility for customers and only few would amalgamate or succeed for the coming centuries. Hard work, commitment, dream and success would be the drivers of business in the future. Hard work is still mandatory for those wonderful scientists and geeks behind the impeccable technologies that we use 25 hours a day. It is needed to at least make the smart apps work for us. Commitment is the thread running through all business houses that have lasted for decades and more to come. Otherwise they would wrap up the show because markets prefer all players with equal interest and commitment drives the best ahead from the worst. Dream drives the crazy, wise and zealots alike. In business world it has to be combined with the hard work and commitment to make it meaningful and up-and-coming business. Success favours the brave. The business professionals who can yearn for success can possess the other qualities and vice versa. Success would embrace the business that shows commitment to customers, hard work in producing products and innovation and dreams of success. The work place ethics would be success. When success becomes ethics, all ingredients are also its accompaniments. Business becomes more than business. Business, more than business means doing a bit extra with employees, going an extra mile with customers, investing for some change beyond returns, and achieving market presence.

Chapter 8

The Last Legion - Business More than Business – Matrix

Every founder establishes concerns with the intention of gaining more than others and passion of changing the world. No firm is founded on less than a dream and dreams are always one notch or several notches above reality. The companies are instruments to achieve something in the name of business. However, in 99% of the companies, their vision stays at sky and operations are grounded to reality. They can hardly break even and hence struggle to level up with maximizing revenues, minimizing costs, handling extra in CSR and upgrading technologies. All business games play around the same dynamics. Winners are those that think out of box. Leaders are companies that can do more than this. It is as simple as it sounds. Business excellence is also not put at such a high benchmark after all, because not all companies can reach there or even try at it. Next century would see a marked change in the business attitude of young generations. The aim would not be to make something for the business but something for the customer. Customers know and act demanding but frankly, no business reaches that expectation, and hence customers adjust their perceptions and expectations. Customer as a human being had always wanted to ease down on the human effort but personal computers advanced much after the long use of heavy big machines. We all want the magic pills or panacea for all ills; this has been true for centuries. But the expectation drills down to overcoming an epidemic and so on. Hence the business research whether in electronics or pharmaceuticals is progressing in its own stead. We achieve as much as business. The attitude of business achievers is still narrow. People don't imagine beyond bounds. As behavioural scientists put it, every age is bound by its own rationalities. An age comes with a capability and expectation, and we feel more than happy if we meet it. The rational is that the overall demands of an age are much more than human bounds can handle. The reality is that there are no human bounds. Sky is the starting point, and universe has lot many areas to limit. This attitude would be the driving force for next century business. Business would not earn profit for itself but for others. It sounds generous but true, now itself the start can be seen. Companies or rather businesses with less known names are working to make something more than profits. Founders are making small yet powerful products to address exactly one need that is getting unnoticed among myriad others. Customers are able to just pay as much as the price of the product yet generates returns out of the business. In future we have to make sure that the output per unit of input has to rise and this is important regardless of technologies or times. The reasons are the rising population, inherent business goals to reach high, rising demand and globalization of business. The efficiency has to be much more than that is today. Past business failures can teach lessons and future business expectations can teach the path of success. Today's business can be handled only by doing business more than business.

More business in terms of productivity, quality, skilled output, commitment to corporate standards, definite strategies for success, reduction of failure rates and galloping pace of technological innovation – and many more, the more your teams can think of – the better it is for you. Whatever more is generated today gets accumulated for future and business reverts itself from complacency in times of success. Also, it helps bail itself out in times of crisis. Different needs flow from all directions at all times. Needs cannot be stopped. Needs are endless. Shareholders ask for higher dividends. Employees ask for promotions, higher salaries and bonuses. Customers ask for lower prices and better offers. Government asks for better compliance and more taxes. Dealers ask for more margins. Hence it is always that we ask for better, more and higher than earlier each time. The only solution is that business does more than business. It does not mean expansion beyond scope or scale, of course if it works, then firms can go ahead. Business is dichotomous. Firms can make both profits and losses out of the same business. Firms sometimes, neither make profits nor losses. Hence more volumes, labor, locations, mergers, products, prices etc. are all on-going. 22nd century is the time for businesses to reach customer's heart. She thinks out of brain but acts out of heart because she loves herself. Businesses must also love customers. Or business must start... How many businesses love their customers? They hardly know who their customers are. KYC or email newsletters are not indicative enough of your involvement with customers. In the auto-generated email world, how many businesses can convince their customers that they know their needs? Unless you know customer, how can you know her needs? How can I guess that a customer called Mia is sitting in a remote corner in Miami and needs a mike that can record while she's talking? Of course, businesses should train their employees, if possible in telepathy. Simultaneously, business houses should start investing **'time'** in getting to know and understand their customers. Who would do that? Employees. They must also be known to the top managers. The top leaders cannot sit back and assign the tasks without even knowing their subordinates' names. It starts right in the company. First know your employees well. Understand them and their capabilities. Fulfil their needs to an extent like perks, incentives, hikes, vacations etc. and then leave them on the fields to hunt and understand customers. Let me reveal the objective. The next century business goal is to partner with customers. Do you enter into joint venture or alliance or M&A without knowing the other company? No. You not only bend your employees' backs in making them crunch and analyse the other party's numbers, data, facts, events, announcements etc., but also take them to dinners and luncheons for getting the formal secrets out in informal places. Don't you divide the line between positives and negatives before making a decision in favour or against? Every firm has fit with SWOT. Strengths and weaknesses go hand-in-hand in every company's history. You still develop trust and go ahead with a venture and you only continue to discover more and more trends and SWOTs by knowing the company's management teams well. The next century, similarly, would handle everything from the customer's perspective. Right from establishment to sales, a customer would be the mother of the company in the next century. Hence you have to love and you would love the customers. A company won't give birth to customers but customers would give birth to companies. The cycle would be end-to-front i.e. end-user to front-office. Employees would need to talk, meet, greet, party and gather with customer(s) because a company is composed of human beings. This is going to be a major job of the next century. Robots can do everything than human can do except understand others' feelings. So far, it has been restricted to books, when we say 'look-and-feel' of the business. The look is in the employees. The feel is in the customers. Just as we stay with our mothers till we grow and leave in her old age, businesses leave their customers once they grow beyond them. The reason could be that the business itself is not capable. How can business be selfish? It can only sell fish. Let customers tell you the stories of their fish in pond or aquarium. Leave the customers in your company. That should be the goal of the businesses. Let customers share their lives with your employees. Talking is the best form of communication that is more spontaneous and direct. Writing is fine but gets influenced by a lot more factors than the individual writing or blogging. Businesses have to become more saintly in using the telepathic forms of communication. I'm not against it. Let businesses recruit some sages and saints on their Boards. I'm sure that they would do the same in the next century. When businessmen can become saints, why can't the reverse be true? Saints can become professionals for guiding the companies to come clean out in the world of bureaucracy and confusion? Chaos cannot last long if great men can help us with what others want. Knowing your customer's problems and averting their life's mishaps would drive your customers crazy to be with you all the time and to yearn for your existence with and for them always. Money is secondary. You won't get a penny if you have no customers. If you have them as your family partners, then you get money in pools. A customer would tell you to start a business for making food for her dog, gives you the ingredients, investment capital, helps you manufacture the same, takes it, and pays you. The next step is even interesting. She helps you in selling it to others like her. Whatever she does or not is her will and wish. A customer is not obliged to do any of the above. Still she wants to do. What more can you ask for? I think that such business would survive for centuries as it bonds on human values directly. It is not as easy as it sounds. Life and business have their problems and ways. The way of business is to get customers into your loop. The way of life is still unknown. Business is equally mysterious. It reveals its own secrets and ways to conduct business along time. You should be able to run the business without realizing the years or time. It is the most enjoyable. You cannot enjoy your business unless your customers do. I'm not sure how many customers enjoy your business though they buy your products. I hardly notice the brand or company name when I get my documents photo-copied. How many of you do? I didn't even know till late in my career that Canon, or HP have their printers along with Xerox. I want to get my task done. How, where, when does not matter to me. May be the other two matter a bit but the first one doesn't even bother me. Or rather who prints? I only know if it is me or my colleague or my peon who would take the papers. How can customers change their style and change the next century business? How can I be so confident? Curiosity. Today we have business centres and life coaching mentors telling that the only way to innovate is to be curious and question everything. Tomorrow this is the only thing to bank upon in the business. How can we do more? Where is our money going? What is the cause for defects in drier while I'm drying my hair just before a meeting? Necessity is the mother of inventions. We don't want any mishap in our lives. Our lives are full of goods. The only way to ensure a happy family is to build bridges with companies. After all, who would take care of our families in our busy schedules and hectic lives? In a way our necessities are creating a curiosity that needs to be redirected in the right way because curiosity kills the cat and we don't want to become cats. Neither can we restrict our curiosity to 9 times. The drastically high levels of output per input would reduce the work hours of employees to

1-2 hours daily. In that case, the employees would be put to the cause of the customers. Every customer would get a relationship manager for every product in every company. It's a furlong extension of what banks today are doing with you. Every employee would spend time visiting a customer alone in San Francisco from South Africa. Every employee would know the name, family tree, and even the inner wishes of customers. Man is free. Business cannot be free but wants to be free. The only way is to befriend customers. Business is shackled in chains of hundreds of complexities and complications that one can think of. There are formalities, tools, rules, policies, conditions, terms, disclaimers, requests, contexts, pretexts, differences, disagreements, regulations, compliances and penalties. Customers won't want any of those. Neither do businesses. One way is to let customers form their own rules so that they abide them. At the same time, they don't let business become boring because if firms become boring, they can't survive. Know customers by their names. The one sector that is going to gain business is the memory training and coaching centres. Employees will be trained in communication skills and behavioural sciences. And as I said earlier, some of us would get trained with reading psyches. This is needed because the increasing mechanization and automation is increasing the distances between a father and a son let alone customer and employee. An employee is a seller. A customer is a buyer. A buyer-seller relationship is not mechanical but definitely tiring one. If it's tiring then it has to be human. Each and every employee would be involved in the task of bridging world between company and customers. Customers forget the company the moment they take the product back home. Only exceptional companies are remembered. But all 22nd century companies want to be known and reputable. Companies can even think of assigning customer's tasks like bill-paying, cleaning garages etc. to employees. I'm not scaring but the list is such that the employees would take care of the task. A well-known General Manager may be busy in hunting for a carpenter to fix the customer's table while she's away at work. Right now, how many of us do our own work? Few... We have servants and maids and machines if not anybody else. Just as we do our work, we have to do customers'. We will do by wish and not force. How many of us don't send reminders for meetings? It's a crude extension of the same. It sounds cheap but so the more sophisticated when you put the time factor of 22nd century when flying cars, speaking robots or virtual offices are not dreams but reality. We have to put up with the times. If we have made the world around us robotic and automated then we have to pay for it. Businesses cannot boast of simply making and launching 50 robots in a police station or bank. They have to get the customers going. The times are not going to be so dark also with familial ties vanishing. The people- the employees of our vendor companies are going to meet us. Robots will interact with us but the matter does not end there. The employee sales rep of the company from whom I used to buy bread wants to know why I've been buying pita for the last 2 weeks and that too from his competitor. A customer who is doing the same may reveal or rather discover only after meeting the rep that she needs corn bread. The rep suggests the same to me and I jump up on the idea. We notify 20 more of our friends on social media posts and now the market is seen shifting towards corn bread. Each and every employee should be a sales person because the task of company is to tell and sell its offerings. Next century would ensure that because I don't need 3 people to work on payrolls. Machines can do that. They might do that one hour daily and devote the rest of the time in meeting and understanding customers. If you have to explain the business to your customer, then no matter what, you would yourself make sure that you know your business inside out. The music of customers is of another impact. It would make you run and work. It soothes you when you are done with the customers' preferences. Otherwise, it would show you the path to slogging, struggle, hard work, sincerity and dedication to win them in the business. Not all customers would be friendly. They are also human beings. The employees would spend hours understanding the feelings of customers, in tacit and expressible forms. A customer would not buy a product if it is not certified or tested. Another customer won't even entertain the company's employee. It takes lot of follow-up and diligent effort to win the trust and confidence of customers, without which the business is of no existence. Such business is lifeless and dead. Companies want to last for decades and not become extinct like dinosaurs. More life into business comes from more business. More business comes from more customers. More customers come from more business and customers. The cycle is infinite. Business of next century would aim at entering this circle of business where it becomes endless. A business can become interminable only if knows its customers not because it can render influence in the community. It can be sure that known customers won't desert it or at least without a notice. New ways of business in customers giving notice before leaving loyalty are not remote. Companies would get time to recompense for losses incurred by customers or mending the ways of business. Only customers who personally know the employees and vice versa would practice such an arrangement. It gives a headlong mileage for the companies without an iota of doubt. Why would customers agree? The answer is in *vice versa* above. Customers may know the employees personally but without any solicited attention from employees. When employees show concern in customers then they would learn a lot about their past, present and future needs that can be correlated to any of the existing complaints with the company's products to bridge the gap. This is a big sentence – in length and meaning. Read between the lines 3-4 times.

Breathe in and breathe out. Don't forget breathing.

Business Management has been managing people, resources, capabilities, technologies, finance, skills, and sorts. In the coming ages, it would essentially be brain management. Mind training is needed in the coming times for all people as global citizens of the world.

Business can succeed with all effort in all times and periods. Business in the ensuing span would be managed by managing people with three key ingredients – trust, affection and fear. All businesses need to have the three though they are not human. Management would succeed if the stakeholders have trust and confidence in one another. Dilute the trust and the whole business goes for a toss. People with brains have confidence and belief in others. Business with such people would also retain some of it. Hence business management in twenty second century would be possible as business with brains. More business means more trust, more affection and more fear. Why fear? The fear of customers, regulators and most of all talent is necessary. When companies fear losing their customers they would be alert and do more for them. As companies grow with regulations, they should not feel complacent and ignore government bodies for fear of losing incentive or penalties. Business is managed on talent of employees; but for the same, business is shallow. Business show is hosted on the talent of stakeholders of that business. When business has the fear of losing the best talent it motivates and trains them in the right stead. We all conduct businesses on the said tenets but now they get distilled amongst myriad others as most relevant ones for the succeeding age. As business stays intact through times, the convergence to success drivers happens and next century would be more like a twisting period for all business. The twist back to the age-old tenets would ensure the perfect revival of human skills in an age of technology. How else can the youngest of generations to come learn about the best business secrets of their ancestors? As civilizations have progressed, we have retained the best and improved upon the worst. Business was nothing when the culture was not in place. The uncivilized era conducted business on totally unconscious levels where the buyer and seller didn't even realize so. Transactions took place on walls and boats with loads of material exchanged without price attached to it. This is the middle age of business. The subsequent century would start the advanced age of business. The trend is clear. Technology is the big brother of business to come. Where else can we work after robotics gains its impetus? Many things would emerge, I'm sure but things would go back and check human progress. So we would definitely work on human brains and training them to the best use of mankind. We have to because of the increasing robotics in life. When robots do all the work, in such cases, who will complete their thinking? We. Why? Why not? Robots can't be let to let down humans to become our masters. Human beings in the form of students, employees and citizens would have to be trained to deal with the business of robotics. Train the trainer to get the best business management. Robots can be allowed to manage business but they have to be managed in turn by humans to avoid havoc and wreck of Matrix or Independence Day or Avatar sorts. In fact they would be the new forms of business slowdowns or crises in the next century. We can't talk of all good things in the next century. Every spell has its own business pitfalls. When robots can't find a match between business needs and goals, they may stretch targets and reek out havoc by burning themselves out. The bosses have to be the human beings in all robotic stages. Hence our minds have to be retained of intelligence and intellect more than the robots.

We have otherwise we can't create one like us or better than us. Robots as subordinates have to be better than human beings. A boss should always hire subordinates who are more intelligent than she. We need to place the intelligence in the right halves of the brain and activate them according to the industry need. If robots are playing business in the education sector then we need to activate the left part of the brain. If robots are pertinent in the creativity sector then the human bosses must activate their right hemisphere of the brain. In summary, we have to retain a higher footing than robots in all businesses. There has to be something of which robots know not a bit and control not a bit. That is human brain. Otherwise business can see the same volatility and misery as of any other times. The mind should be the terminator when need arises. Robots can possess mind because it is the invisible matter with research-in-motion for eternity. Business of next century can be facilitated with the help of robots or clones. Clones of unions or labourer can be launched for handling skill tasks which are physically quite demanding. Groups of cloned workmen can be created for handling the specific tasks, whose productivity can thus be increased. In many ways, the business of next century would shackle our minds to create a goal-centric individual everywhere. The education and business would be pre-decided, and even the birth of that individual.

There would be multiple facets of life but not as varied as now. Today business is already seen as a constricting field that is eating away all time and activity. People don't get time to be with kids. They are missing out on lot of activities like games and feats that were hitherto part of our ancestors.

Life would be largely driven by business in the next century and not vice versa. The economy would identify the industry needs in terms of number of doctors, engineers, pilots, teachers, et al along with the number of hospitals, aircraft, schools, students, patients, et al. The whole world would be planned to conspire for the business. Business management hence would be planned too. The families would be analysed according to parental gene and the offspring would be planned to have specific skills for handling a given business role. A police cop would be born on Day 1 and trained in life for the same. In the process, a lot of other things relevant to human life would be missed or skipped. There would be a sophisticated techno-human life for strategic-humans. I'm calling them strategic-humans because they are born for business cause by following a strategy for life. The genes would be deactivated as per need and may have the option of enabling them if the child wants to deviate from the business plan. The human minds would be freed of lot of activities to just manage the intellect part to guide the future centuries' business or life. A key question emerges with irony. Where are we heading? All attention goes back to the beginning point where the invisible force started being searched for and today called as God, mind or nature. Business converges with humanity thus again.

www.ingramcontent.com/pod-product-compliance
Lightning Source LLC
Chambersburg PA
CBHW070243190526
45169CB00001B/291

9 781534 868939